Kreinik

METALLIC THREAD
Embroidery

Kreinik
METALLIC THREAD Embroidery

A Practical Guide to Stitching Creatively with
Metallic Threads

Jacqueline Friedman Kreinik
and
Ann Caswell
(Design Co-ordinator)

David & Charles

To all embroiderers around the world, who, with deep passion, a love for
beauty and a desire for self-expression, use simple tools to
create works of wonder. I congratulate you all.

A DAVID & CHARLES BOOK

First published in the UK in 2000

Text and designs Copyright © Kreinik Manufacturing Company, Inc. 2000

Photography and layout Copyright © David & Charles 2000

Jacqueline Friedman Kreinik has asserted her right to be identified as author of this work

in accordance with the Copyright, Designs and Patents Act, 1988.

A catalogue record for this book is available from the British Library.

ISBN 0 7153 1081 X

Photography by David Johnson

Book design by Diana Knapp

Printed in Hong Kong by Dai Nippon for David & Charles

Brunel House   Newton Abbot   Devon

CONTENTS

INTRODUCTION

THE IDEA FOR WRITING *METALLIC THREAD EMBROIDERY* WAS FIRST AND FOREMOST A RESPONSE TO THE INQUIRIES RECEIVED FROM YOU, THE STITCHER. ALWAYS SEARCHING FOR ANSWERS AND NEW DIRECTIONS, KREINIK'S MISSION TO HELP STITCHERS UNDERSTAND THE WHY, WHEN AND HOW OF USING METALLIC THREADS RESULTED IN THIS BOOK. WE WANTED TO EXPLAIN THE SIGNIFICANCE OF METAL AND METALLIC THREADS IN EMBROIDERY AND TO CREATE A GLOSSARY OF TERMS TO HELP ESTABLISH A COMMON LANGUAGE FOR USING METALLIC THREADS. FINALLY, WE WANTED TO EXPAND THE CREATIVE OPTIONS THAT STITCHERS HAVE AT THEIR FINGERTIPS BY ILLUSTRAT-ING THE POSSIBILITIES THROUGH THE DESIGNS IN CHAPTER 4, AND BY HELPING NEEDLEWORKERS ENJOY STITCHING MORE THOROUGHLY.

THE SIGNIFICANCE OF METAL THREADS

METALLIC AND METAL THREADS are some of the most interesting and useful materials available to needleworkers today. These threads add beautiful and dramatic effects to even a simple design. The use of real metal threads in embroidery is believed to date back as far as 3,000 BC. Gold embellishment on fabric was revered for its unique beauty and visual impact. Whether used in Ancient Egypt, Europe or the Orient, metal thread in textile decoration owed its importance to the symbolic significance attached to gold. Gold has always had meaning and value for all people in all societies, the main reason for this being that gold symbolically represents the sun.

The sun, with its light-giving properties, was perceived during early civilisations to possess special powers. Our ancestors knew that all things were connected with the sun: plants, animals, seasons, weather, agriculture, life and death. What we see and perceive are the result of the sun's light. It was not surprising, therefore, that the sun was celebrated and revered; in fact, most religious rituals, social functions, festivities and sports can be traced back to the ancient worship of the sun.

Gold quickly became the sun's metal. Its colour, malleability and the fact that it does not tarnish, made it an appropriate medium for solar imagery. Silver, and to a lesser degree copper and bronze, have also shared light imagery in artistic uses, but incorporating gold threads into textiles has challenged the craftsperson since ancient times and continues to challenge all needleworkers today.

THE EMERGENCE OF METALLIC THREADS

While the words 'metal' and 'metallic' are often used interchangeably, the two terms do not have the same meaning. To be a true 'metal', the greatest percentage of the thread must be either a metal or a metal compound. A metal or metal compound is flattened, cut into very fine strips and then wrapped around a silk, cotton or linen core. The expertise, materials, and cost required to create real metal threads make them a rarity for embroiderers today.

In the 1950s and 1960s, technological advances permitted manufacturers to make less expensive threads as substitutes for real metal threads. Those synthetic metallic threads were easier to use than metal threads, more affordable and readily available. Unfortunately, they were stiff, limited in colour to gold and silver and limited, too, in their use in hand embroidery.

The term 'metallic' is correctly applied to all threads that appear to be made of metal but are actually composed of a synthetic material such as polyester plated with a thin layer of metal, which is lacquered to protect it and provide colours. With the continuing improvement of technologies in thread manufacturing, metallic threads have gained widespread acceptance among needleworkers. Now, because of their soft feel, wide colour range and attractive appearance, metallic threads have taken on a life of their own, adding texture, dimension and visual excitement to all types of needlework.

Adding metallic threads to a design enables stitchers to bring visual realism to needlework. Metallic threads have innate properties that allow them to hold and reflect light, thus creating a light source in a design. By using metallic threads the possibilities for creating vibrant, true-to-life needlework become endless. Considering that metallic threads can represent sunlight, artificial light, moonlight or starlight, needleworkers can recreate colour, contrast and even movement to bring life to a design: snow glistens, flowers become dew-covered, a hummingbird looks iridescent, even fairy dust gleams and angels' wings magically sparkle. Simply by including metallic threads in a design, the stitcher can change a flat, one-dimensional piece into a multi-dimensional, visually diverse work of art.

THE ♕ Kreinik STORY

The story of Kreinik Manufacturing Co., Inc. is as much a story of determination, product knowledge, vision and love as it is of product creation.

In 1971, at the age of fifty-six, Jerry Kreinik, a textile and chemical engineer and scientist, was caught in the early phase of the downswing trend among chemical manufacturers. While living in Parkersburg, West Virginia, Jerry drove around the eastern part of the United States looking for a job. His wife, Estelle, accompanied him, taking her stitching along for the long stretches of road between interviews.

As time passed, Estelle, a clothing and textile assistant professor and ardent needlewoman, eventually spread her needlework projects throughout the car. Jerry, finding the threads an inch up to his waist, asked if she could develop some way to contain the threads. So Estelle designed and made the first portable carrying case for her threads, needles, needlework canvases and accessories. The design, called 'PAKKS', so delighted them and their friends that Estelle started sewing carrying cases in her home and Jerry began to sell them as he travelled for business. They got re-orders and Kreinik Manufacturing Company began in 1972.

A NEW DIRECTION

While he was travelling and selling the carrying cases and an assortment of needlework canvases, Jerry studied the selections of yarns and threads available in shops. Both Jerry and Estelle had long been students of art and textile history: Jerry gave lectures on the clothing of Chaucer's characters and Estelle taught aeronautical organisations about the role of textiles in the development and progress of space travel.

Their knowledge of historical textiles made them realise the selection of threads available at the time was limited and did not reflect the wide range of threads that had been used in needlework in the past. Historically, needleworkers from Egypt, China and many European countries incorporated different types of thread into their work because the contrast provided by the lustre of these materials enriched the designs. Silk, wool, linen, cotton and metal threads were combined to convey a sense of texture and depth, making the finished piece more appealing and life-like.

After the Second World War, many embroiderers used only one type of thread in their projects (cotton for cross stitch and wool for needlepoint) because of economic conditions and product availability. This omission of different types of threads resulted in designs that were beautiful, yet lacked the realism and visual interest that a contrast among threads creates. This contrast results in texture and dimension.

Noticing this void, Jerry and Estelle began to develop specifications for new kinds of threads to introduce to the market in the late 1970s. Among these was a unique line of soft, colourful and easy-to-use synthetic metallic threads that were hand and machine washable and dry-cleanable. In the beginning these metallic threads came in three sizes and fifteen colours and were introduced under the name Balger®, a registered trademark of Kreinik Manufacturing Company, Inc.

A SECOND GENERATION

Seventeen years ago, their son Douglas joined Estelle and Jerry in the business. He worked in production and co-ordinated the computerisation of the company. He and Jerry also installed new machinery, which expanded the production capabilities. Thirteen years ago, son Andrew and his wife Jacqueline joined the business. Andrew came to oversee administrative affairs, while Jacqueline took charge of the marketing and educational programs. Ten years ago, Douglas, Andrew and Jacqueline purchased the business and expanded it.

The selection of metallic threads has now grown to 17 types and over 160 colours. To ease the consumer's search for the threads, they are all marketed under the name Kreinik, a name that has become known for innovation and quality. Today the Kreinik family still works closely together to insure that the innovation in thread development continues.

## chapter 1

THE KREINIK THREADS

KREINIK METALLIC THREADS ARE SOME OF THE MOST INTERESTING AND USEFUL MATERIALS AVAILABLE TO EMBROIDERERS TODAY. WHETHER THE ART FORM IS CROSS STITCH, NEEDLEPOINT, CROCHET, GOLD WORK, MACHINE EMBROIDERY, CRAFTS OR OTHER TECHNIQUES, METALLIC THREADS ADD BEAUTIFUL AND DRAMATIC EFFECTS TO EVEN SIMPLE DESIGNS. METALLIC THREADS REFLECT LIGHT TO A HIGHER DEGREE THAN MATT THREADS, OFFERING A UNIQUE PLAY ON COLOUR. THIS UNIQUE PLAY OF LIGHT ON COLOUR IS WHAT MAKES THE EMBROIDERY MORE VISUALLY APPEAL-ING AND EXCITING. THE METALLIC THREADS ARE NOT INTENDED TO REPLACE COTTON, WOOL OR SILK, BUT TO CREATE A CONTRAST IN TEXTURE AND DIMENSION, OR IN COLOUR AND LIGHT REFLECTION, WHICH ENHANCES THE OVERALL EFFECT OF A DESIGN.

KREINIK THREAD TYPES

EACH TYPE OF KREINIK METALLIC THREAD 'sits' on the surface of an embroidery differently, offering variations in depth, height or dimension. Combine a twisted metallic braid with smooth silk, or a matt cotton with a glossy metallic and look at the way the threads work together to make a design appear more lifelike. Each thread type has multiple applications and can be used to achieve various effects. Knowing the types of metallic threads available and understanding how, why, where and when they are used, will enable you to select the appropriate threads to enhance a design (see Selection Chart, page 21).

As any stitcher can relate, different types of stitchery require different sizes and types of threads. As a result, Kreinik produces seventeen different types of metallic threads (see some examples below). Each type of thread has a feel, appearance or texture that is different from another. Refer to the Selection Chart (page 21), Thread Guide (page 13), and Colour Chart (page 120) for help in selecting the appropriate sizes and colours of metallic threads for your projects. Refer also to Needle Selection on page 25 for help in choosing needle sizes for metallic threads.

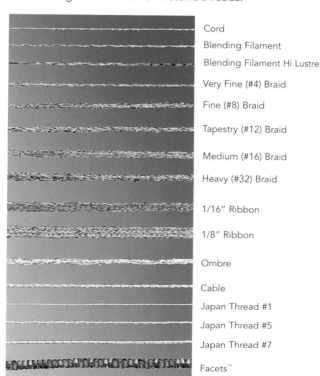

Cord
Blending Filament
Blending Filament Hi Lustre

Very Fine (#4) Braid

Fine (#8) Braid

Tapestry (#12) Braid

Medium (#16) Braid

Heavy (#32) Braid

1/16" Ribbon

1/8" Ribbon

Ombre

Cable

Japan Thread #1

Japan Thread #5

Japan Thread #7

Facets™

THREAD TEXTURAL STYLES

There are five textural styles found in Kreinik Metallic Threads – Basic, Hi-Lustre, Glow-in-the-Dark, Vintage and Cord. Depending on the base material used, the metallic threads have different textures and degrees of light reflection.

Basic refers to a slightly twisted, round thread that has a subtle sheen when used alone or combined with another thread. When made into Kreinik Braids and Ribbons, it has a moderate lustre. Basic threads are identified by numbers, as in 002 Gold.

Hi-Lustre refers to a flat metallic thread that has a highly reflective nature. This thread type is identified with an 'HL' after the colour number, as in 002HL. Hi-Lustre threads in Kreinik Braids and Ribbons have a bold and glossy appearance.

Glow-in-the-Dark refers to a flat thread that has a subtle glow when exposed to light. Glow-in-the-Dark threads create a magical effect, adding sparkle to stars, moisture to tropical fish, illumination to Hallowe'en motifs, and a glow to children's projects or any whimsical design. A moon stitched in these threads will emit a soft glow when the lights dim. The length of time the material will glow depends upon the length of time it is exposed to direct light. For example, five minutes of direct light equals approximately ten to fifteen minutes of glow time. The threads are ideal for decorating clothing, but should not be used as a substitute for safety-rated reflective material for visibility at night. This thread type is identified with an 'F' after the colour number, as in 051F.

Vintage describes a flat thread with an antique matt finish. It has a muted metallic appearance, and is identified with a 'V' following the colour number, as in 002V.

Cord has a tight metallic wrapping around the core. It is strong, durable and has a high metallic sheen. When made into Kreinik corded braids and corded ribbons, it has a 'nubby' texture, similar to the look of a real metal thread. These threads are identified with a 'C' following the colour number, as in 007C.

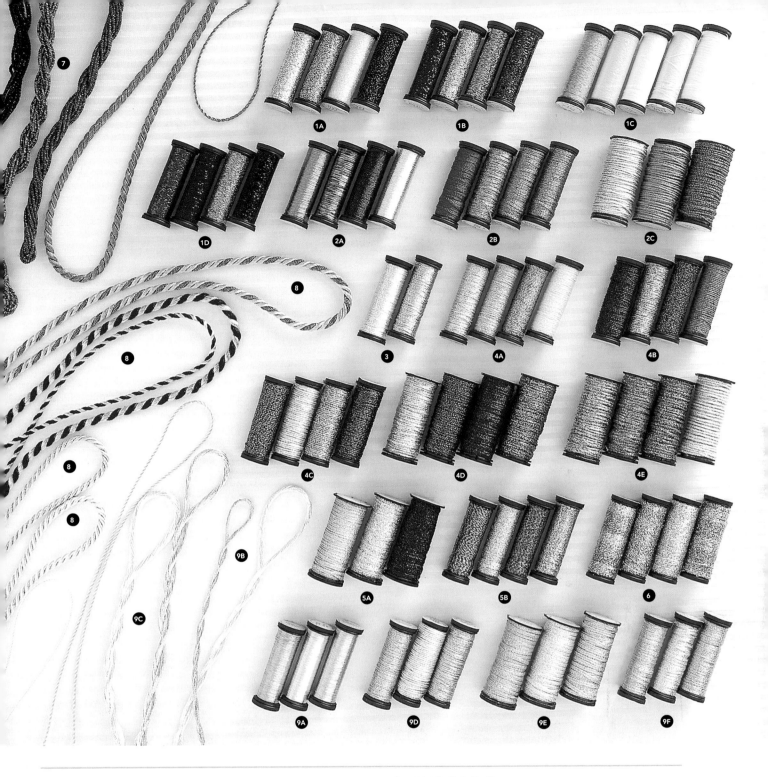

KREINIK METALLIC THREADS

Blending Filament
- **1A** Basic
- **1B** Hi-Lustre
- **1C** Glow-in-the-Dark
- **1D** Vintage

Cord
- **2A** Cord (single-strand)
- **2B** Corded Ribbon
- **2C** Corded Braid
- **3** Cable

Braid
- **4A** Very Fine (#4)
- **4B** Fine (#8)
- **4C** Tapestry (#12)
- **4D** Medium (#16)
- **4E** Heavy (#32)

Ribbon
- **5A** ⅛" Ribbon
- **5B** ¹⁄₁₆" Ribbon
- **6** Ombre
- **7** Facets™
- **8** Torsades

Japan Threads
- **9A** #1 (Super Fine)
- **9B** #5 (Fine)
- **9C** #7 (Medium)
- **9D** Japan Braids
- **9E** Japan Ribbons ⅛"
- **9F** Japan Ribbons ¹⁄₁₆"

THREAD TYPES AND USES

BLENDING FILAMENT

Blending Filament is a thin, single-ply metallic thread that can be used alone or combined with other threads and yarns in the same needle to produce a subtle sheen. It is composed of a polyester metallic thread with a supporting core; it is not recommended that you remove the support core from the metallic thread. All the Blending Filaments can easily be threaded on to the needle for easier control by using the technique illustrated on page 24.

The filaments are perfect for enhancing needlepoint, cross stitch and embroidery designs. Blending Filament is also popular for punch embroidery, lace making, weaving, knitting, crochet and machine sewing. It is available in an assortment of more than seventy-five colours and in four colour types: Basic, Hi-lustre, Glow-in-the-Dark and Vintage. Please refer to the Metallic Thread Colour Chart on pages 120–121 to view the colours.

Because Blending Filament is thin and does not add weight to the stitches, it allows the stitcher to determine how much highlight, reflection or shimmer is wanted in the design. Contrast is created when you mix different materials – for example, cotton, wool or silk – together with the Blending Filament. This gives the project more visual excitement and realism. There are many different ways to use the filaments – alone, single strand, doubled, or combined with other thread types.

Basic Blending Filaments These are blended in the needle with cotton in cross stitches to add highlights, as in the hummingbird and flowers in Flight of Nature (page 46). Basic Blending Filaments are used single strand in a half cross stitch to create soft, shimmery backgrounds as shown in Angelic Messenger (page 60), and Dragonfly Illusion (page 64 and the picture detail below). In many of the projects, filaments are combined with stranded cotton (floss) or silk to create various special effects.

Flat Blending Filaments Hi-Lustre, Glow-in-the-Dark and Vintage may be treated as tiny ribbons. Care must be

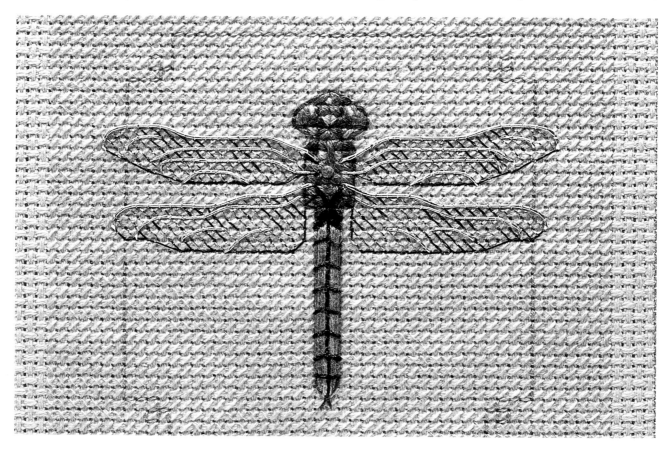

taken to lay these threads smoothly in place to allow maximum light reflection. Use your finger or a laying tool to prevent them from twisting as you stitch.

Combining Blending Filament with Other Threads Gentle, consistent tension is important when stitching with Blending Filament and will ensure easy handling of the thread. It is recommended that you secure Blending Filament in the eye of the needle before combining it with another type of thread, using the needle threading technique on page 24. You may wish to moisten the

filament together with the other thread using a slightly damp, soft cosmetic sponge. These techniques help to control both thread types as they work together in your needle.

Overstitching Overstitching is a technique using Blending Filament or other fine thread, to stitch on top of a particular area or design element in order to enhance or accent it. For example, an eye stitched in stranded cotton (floss) may be highlighted by adding a stitch of pearl or white Blending Filament on top of the already stitched pupil. Reflective highlights may also be added to areas of sunlight, moonlight, water or dew by overstitching with Blending Filament.

Blending filament is a perfect companion to stranded cotton (floss), their different characteristics working very well together

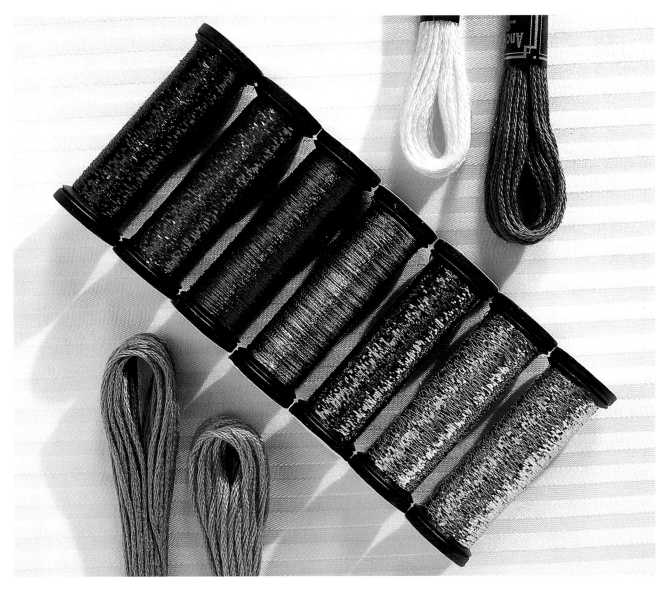

CORD

Cord is a single-strand thread that has a metallic covering tightly wrapped over a core (gimp). It has a rich metallic colour that brings definition to designs. This single-strand thread is ideal for outlining on fabric. When backstitched around a motif, for example, the thin, clean line visually lifts the element off the fabric and creates a sense of dimension. It is also excellent for blackwork-style stitchery, 'lacy' effects, and openwork on fabric. In addition, you can also use a single strand of Cord to overstitch areas on fabric or canvas, bringing exacting definition to designs. The thin and strong qualities of Cord make it ideal for couching thicker Kreinik Braids and Ribbons. Match colours of Cord to the thread you are couching to remain invisible, or use a different colour to create interesting contrasts. If you enjoy creating the look of gold work, use gold (or silver) colours of Cord to couch real metal threads or corded braids and ribbons.

Cord is used to make Kreinik corded braids and corded ribbons. These heavier threads also carry a 'C' after the colour number and they have a nubby, real-metal appearance. In the design, Flight of Nature (page 46), Nickel Cord was used for all the outlining which visually lifts the design elements off the surface, creating a sense of dimension. Cord was used to couch various sizes of Braid in Rhapsody of Lace (see page 56 and the picture detail below), again to create dimension. A beautiful pattern was developed by

the designer of the Regency Stocking (page 112) using Cord to overstitch satin stitch blocks.

Some stitchers prefer to use the threading technique shown on page 24 when using the single strand Cord, to prevent the thread from sliding out of the needle. Stitch slowly with Cord to achieve more control.

CORDED BRAID

The Corded Braids are constructed of four or more single-strand cords braided together, generating a wonderful selection of different sized dimensional and textured round threads. Corded Braids are increasingly being used in place of real metal threads because they closely resemble them and are less costly. They are available in Very Fine (#4), Fine (#8), Tapestry (#12), or Medium (#16) which may be used in the body of a design or to create a cloisonné-style outline. Corded Braids are also excellent for tassels. Very Fine (#4) Corded Braid was used in Rhapsody of Lace (page 56) to accentuate an innovative couching treatment which separates the central field from the border.

CORDED RIBBON

These are flat ribbons made by braiding single-strand cords together. Use the Corded Ribbons couched with a corresponding colour of Cord to create the appearance of elegant gold work. Corded Ribbon is available in ⅛" (3mm) and ¹⁄₁₆" (1.5mm) widths. The Buttercup Bouquet (page 68) uses ¹⁄₁₆" Corded Ribbon for the French knot 'sprinkles' which surround the bouquet, demonstrating the flexibility of the ribbon.

CABLE

Cable is a three-ply, gently twisted cord used most often to create outlines and borders. Available in gold and silver, it is ideal for creating background patterns on canvas. On fabric, it is often used for decorative stitches or outlines, as in samplers. Resembling a real metal thread, it has a classic elegance and refined appearance. It was used to create the lovely border which defines the Romance Sampler (page 71).

For easier control, gently stroke the Cable with your hands before stitching to relax the threads. Stitch slowly and attentively to maintain Cable's soft twist.

BRAID

Braid is made by combining multiple strands of Blending Filament together. It is very easy to control, is strong, lustrous, round in shape, provides excellent coverage and will not ravel. Braid is used alone rather than combined in the needle with other threads. Trims made of Braid are excellent for ornaments or, when multiple braids are twisted together, as trims for larger projects such as pillows. Braids can act as a fillet when framing. A fillet is the piece of moulding, frequently gold or silver, which lies between the frame and the picture. A border stitched with Braid can act as a fillet and nestle up close to the frame to be the perfect complement to all framed embroidery. Braid is available in sizes Very Fine (#4), Fine (#8), Tapestry (#12), Medium (#16) and Heavy (#32). Use the Selection

A variety of different thicknesses and colours are offered in round Braids and flat Ribbons for the different size grounds

Chart on page 21 to help choose the appropriate size for your project.

Braids may be moistened with a slightly dampened cosmetic sponge after removal from the spool to help relax the thread and reduce twisting and knotting.

Examples of the many effects possible with the Braids are contained in various projects in the book. The wetness of the rain is wonderfully depicted on the yellow rain hat and coat in Spring Patchwork Girl (page 90) by using Tapestry (#12) Braid 091 Star Yellow. The Celestial Mobile (page 106) shows the whimsical effect possible with Glow-in-the-Dark Braids.

RIBBONS

Ribbons are amazing metallic threads, made by combining multiple strands of Blending Filament. They are available in ⅛" (3mm) and ⅟₁₆" (1.5mm) widths and are flat, soft, durable and flexible. Because of this, they lay flat on straight or curved surfaces, bending easily without buckling. Laying these ribbons maximises the visual effect of the threads. They are also excellent for trimming edges, binding edges, whipstitching or overcasting edges to give a professional appearance. Ribbons are easy to lay flat with your finger, but a laying tool can be used for extra control.

The Buttercup Bouquet (see page 68 and the picture detail below) shows how well Ribbons perform in the curved and looped stitches of ribbon embroidery. The use of Ribbons in the Classic Golden Balantine (page 84) shows the versatility of using them flat against the surface in canvas embroidery. In one area a Ribbon is couched with a Cord, in another area two different Ribbons are used in the same stitch.

OMBRE

Ombre is a softly twisted, eight-ply metallic thread, ideal for cross stitch, needlepoint, crochet, knitting and machine sewing. Ombre has a soft touch and a smooth, flowing drape which makes it suitable for clothes, purses or table linens. It is available in nine variegated colours as well as solid Gold, Silver and Pearl. Due to Ombre's loose twist, it looks almost 'furry,' which leads to exciting textural possibilities. In canvas work, for example, use it in a variety of stitches for snow, or a garland on a Christmas tree. It is lovely in a satin stitch on fabric or canvas; use a solid colour or take advantage of the variegated shades.

The leaves stitched in Ombre in Autumn Patchwork Girl (see picture detail below) look as if they were kissed by afternoon sunlight. French knots stitched with Ombre were used to create the look of fur for the hat brim, cuff, and coat hem for the Winter Patchwork Girl on page 97.

FACETS™

This bead-like thread can be easily couched by hand or machine to create texture and dimension. When couched it resembles strings of finely cut gems or beads. Place a piece of cellophane tape around the Facets™ where you are cutting it to prevent it from ravelling. Cut through the centre of the piece of tape. Use an awl or a large tapestry needle to gently enlarge places in the ground material in which to plunge the beginning and end of the strands (see couching techniques on page 37).

Facets™ add a touch of elegance to outlines, borders, wearables and home decoration. The frames which surround each of the Four Seasons Patchwork Girls are formed by couching silver Facets™ with silver Cord.

JAPAN THREADS

Japan Threads are synthetic gimps (wrapped threads) with a real silver content that gives the threads an appearance of real metal thread (see picture below). They are available in Gold, Dark Gold, Silver and Copper. These threads have long been admired for the traditional beauty and grace they bring to needlework and are excellent for fine stitching, outlining, couching and laid work. They are available in Super Fine (#1), a stitching thread, Fine (#5) and Medium (#7), both laying threads. Japan Threads are also available in Very Fine (#4), Fine (#8), Tapestry (#12) and Medium (#16) Braids, ⅟₁₆″ and ⅛″ Ribbons.

Japan #1, which is available on a reel, may be used as a stitching thread, but Japan #5 and #7 should not be used to stitch in and out of fabric or canvas but rather be attached to the surface of an embroidery by couching. Japan #5 and #7 are available in skein form.

The richness and elegance of the Japan Threads is beautifully displayed in the Regency Stocking on page 112. They were also used in the framework for the delicate wings in Dragonfly Illusion (see picture on page 14).

The uniques characteristics of Japan threads, Facets™, Ombre and ⅛″ Ribbon give them the ability to create dimensional embroidery with texture and visual appeal

TORSADES

Torsades are twisted cord trims that may be attached to the surface of an embroidery or used as trims to add an elegant embellishment for fashion, surface embroidery and home decor. These rope-style trims are available in solid gold and silver shades and combinations of colourful solids blended with metallic gold and silver. Each colour selection is available in a variety of thicknesses ranging from 1mm to 4mm (see picture, right).

The ends of the Torsades are plunged to the back of the embroidery in much the same manner as couched threads. (See couching techniques, page 37.) Because of their thickness, it is helpful to slightly fan the ends to make threading the eye of the needle easier. Enlarging the canvas hole with an awl or a large tapestry or rug needle prior to plunging also helps to ease the Torsade to the reverse side. Once the tail has been pulled through to the reverse side, give it a slight twist to realign any threads that may have become untwisted on the right side.

A gold Torsade was used to frame the outline and halo of the Friendship Angel on page 101. A silver Torsade was used in the finishing of Sleeping Mermaid and Rainbow Fishes on page 80 to frame the piece.

SILK MORI®

Kreinik Silk Mori® is a six strand, 100 per cent pure, premium spun silk with a creamy lustre. Silk Mori® offers a luxurious sheen and smoothness that is unattainable with stranded cotton (floss), which your fingers will love.

Because Silk Mori® is a multi-strand thread it should be separated before use and the appropriate number of strands recombined before threading the needle. Separating the strands and using a laying tool to keep them parallel, smooth and untwisted during stitching allows for the greatest amount of light reflection. Stitching with Silk Mori® is easier than stitching with stranded cotton (floss).

Silk, like all threads, can become abraded by the constant motion of going through the ground material. You can minimise this abrasion by using working lengths of silk of approximately 38–46cm (15–18in), and using the largest needle possible which does not permanently distort the ground fabric or canvas.

A selection of sumptuous Torsades

SELECTION CHART FOR KREINIK METALLIC THREADS

NAME	TYPE	APPLICATIONS
Blending Filaments	1 Ply Basic Colours Hi Lustre, Vintage & Glow-in-the-Dark	Needlepoint, Embroidery, Cross Stitch, Punch Embroidery, Lace Making, Weaving, Knitting, Crochet, Machine Embroidery. Each type can be used by itself or in combination with other yarns
Cord	1 Ply Gimp	Outlining, Fine Cross Stitch, Brazilian and Machine Embroidery, Quilting, Smocking, Macrame
Cable	3 Ply Twist	Outlining and Fine Cross Stitch, Surface Stitchery
Braids	Very Fine (#4)	Needlepoint (18-30 Canvas), Cross Stitch (14-18 Aida), Smocking, Tatting, Crochet, Embroidery, Machine Sewing, Embroidery, Quilting
	Fine (#8)	Needlepoint (18-30 Canvas), Cross Stitch (14 & 16), Smocking, Weaving, Tatting, Embroidery, Machine Sewing, Brazilian Embroidery and Plastic Canvas (14 count)
	Tapestry™ (#12)	Needlepoint (14-30 Canvas), Cross Stitch (11-16) Smocking, Tatting, Embroidery, Crochet, Machine Sewing, Brazilian Embroidery, Quilting
	Medium (#16)	Needlepoint (14-18 Canvas), Cross Stitch (11-14 Aida), Weaving, Tatting, Embroidery, Crochet, and Trimming, Plastic Canvas (14 count)
	Heavy (#32)	Needlepoint (10-14 Canvas), Cross Stitch (8 & 11 Aida), Trims, Crochet, Macrame, Plastic Canvas (7-10 count)
Ribbons	⅛" Braided Ribbon	Needlepoint (10-18 Canvas), Trims, Crochet, Sewing, Knitting, Weaving, Trim for Miniatures, Plastic Canvas (7-10 count)
	¹⁄₁₆" Braided Ribbon	Needlepoint (18-24 Canvas), Cross Stitch, Knitting, Trims, Embroidery, Machine Embroidery, Applique, Crochet, Plastic Surface Canvas (10-14 count)
Kreinik Ombre	8 Ply	Needlepoint, Machine Knitting, Crochet, Cross Stitch (plies can be separated)
Kreinik Japan Threads	1, 5, 7	Needlepoint, Cross Stitch, Surface Embroidery, Smocking, Quilting, Weaving, Couching

CARE

Kreinik Blending Filaments, Cords, Cables, Braids and Braided Ribbons are <u>hand and machine washable</u> and <u>dry-cleanable.</u> When ironing a finished piece containing Kreinik Metallics do not iron directly on the metallic. Use a press cloth. <u>Do not</u> use steam.

## chapter 2

BASIC TECHNIQUES

STITCHING THE DESIGNS THAT ARE FEATURED IN CHAPTER 4 IS EASY, PLEASURABLE AND CREATIVELY SATISFYING. TO GAIN THE MAXIMUM ENJOYMENT AND SUCCESS FROM THIS BOOK, PLEASE READ THE INFORMATION AND BASIC TECHNIQUES IN THIS CHAPTER CAREFULLY BEFORE EMBARKING ON ANY OF THE PROJECTS. THIS CHAPTER WILL GIVE YOU INVALUABLE ADVICE ON USING METALLIC THREADS AND HOW TO PRODUCE BEAUTIFUL, HIGH-QUALITY EMBROIDERY WITH THEM. THERE IS INFORMATION ON SELECTING THE RIGHT NEEDLE, ON CHOOSING AND USING DIFFERENT FABRICS AND HOW TO ADAPT AND ENHANCE PAINTED (PRE-PRINTED) CANVASES WITH METALLIC THREADS. THERE ARE PRACTICAL REMINDERS ON HOW TO PREPARE YOUR FABRIC FOR WORK, HOW TO START AND FINISH NEATLY AND A WEALTH OF USEFUL STITCHING TIPS.

WORKING WITH METALLIC THREADS

WORKING WITH METALLIC THREADS is as easy as working with plain threads such as stranded cotton (floss), and the following section gives some handy tips on using them.

REMOVING THREAD FROM SPOOLS

Kreinik uses two unique types of spools to hold the threads – the snap spool and the flange lock spool.

The snap spool is used for Blending Filament, Cord, Cable, Very Fine (#4), Fine (#8) and Tapestry (#12) Braid, 1/16" Ribbon, Ombre, and Japan #1. Both sides of the spool open – look for the side where the thread end is located. Insert your thumb nail in the grove under the cap (Fig 1), and rotate the spool while gently lifting the cap to release the thread (the cap shouldn't pop off). Snap the lid down to secure the unused portion.

Fig 1 The open/close snap spool mechanism

The lock flange mechanism is used for the Medium (#16) Braid, Heavy (#32) Braid and 1/8" Ribbon. The heavier thread sizes 'lock' in the groove around the top of the spool (Fig 2). Simply pull the thread to release. Wrap the thread in the groove to secure the unused portion.

Fig 2 The lock flange mechanism

To open a skein of Japan threads #5 or #7   Hold the skein by the loop with one hand and gently pull off the paper label, retaining the label for future reference. Hold the skein and insert one or two fingers into the loop end that does not have the knot. Separate the twisted threads by running your finger slowly down the middle and gently pulling them apart. Lay the skein on a table and untie the loose knot located at one end. Insert your finger in the loop at the end opposite the loosened knot. Place your other hand in the centre beneath the loop and very slowly separate the twisted threads. Cut the threads at one end and then use the appropriate length for your stitchery. The remaining thread should not be folded or creased but loosely wrapped in acid-free tissue paper for storage.

THREADING METALLIC THREADS

Threading Blending Filaments and Cords   To thread Blending Filament and Cord, cut the required length and fold about 5cm (2in) from one end. Insert the loop through the eye of the needle and pull the loop over the point of the needle. Tighten the loop at the end of the eye to secure the thread to the needle (Figs 3a–d).

Fig 3a Loop the thread, pass the loop through the eye of the needle, leaving a short tail

Fig 3b Pull the loop over the point of the needle

Fig 3c Tighten the loop at the end of the eye

Fig 3d Gently stroke the knotted thread once to 'lock' it in place

Threading Metallic Braids and Ribbons To thread Braids and Ribbons, cut a small strip of paper and fold it in half. Place the fold through the eye of the needle and open out the two ends to insert the thread between them. Gently pull the paper through so the thread is brought with it (Fig 4).

Fig 4 Use a strip of folded paper to pull Braids and Ribbons through the eye of the needle

DEALING WITH THREAD FRICTION

Threads, whether metallic, silk, cotton, linen or wool, are most vulnerable when they are passing through the ground material as repeated friction between the thread and ground material damages all threads. To avoid this damage, stitch slowly and use a needle large enough to open the hole in the fabric sufficiently to reduce the friction. Select a needle that will comfortably accommodate the thread but will not permanently distort the ground as you stitch. The enlarged hole is not permanent and will not damage your ground fabric yet this will allow the thread to pass through more easily (see Needle Selection, below).

Thread friction can also be lessened by proper preparation of the ground material, such as covering the edges of embroidery canvas with tape and trimming the edges of plastic canvas smooth.

NEEDLE SELECTION

Choose the largest needle possible for your embroidery so the thread passes easily through the fabric or canvas. The two types of needles used for the projects in the book have either sharp or blunt tips. Sharp tipped needles are generally used on fabric. Blunt tipped needles are used on evenweave fabric and canvas.

Beading needles These are fine and straight with a long, thin eye; they are also flexible which helps in stacking beads onto the needle.

Between or quilting needles Used for sewing, quilting, and embroidery, these needles have a sharp tip and are short with a slit eye.

Crewel or embroidery needles These needles also have a sharp tip but are longer and thinner with a larger slit eye.

Tapestry needles Used for counted or canvas embroidery, these needles have a blunt tip, enabling them to slip through fabric and canvas without piercing the threads.

Sharps needles These are general sewing needles.

If threads routinely fray or snag in your needle, the inside of the eye of the needle may have become damaged and the rough edges of the metal can cause harm to the thread. Discard the old needle.

The table below gives some specific suggestions for choosing needle sizes.

NEEDLE SELECTION

Thread Size	Suggested Needle Size
◆ Heavy (#32) Braid	Tapestry No.18/20
◆ ⅛" Ribbon	Tapestry No.18/20/22
◆ 1⁄16" Ribbon	Tapestry No.22/24
◆ Medium (#16) Braid	Tapestry No.20/22
◆ Tapestry (#12) Braid	Tapestry No.22/24
◆ Fine (#8) Braid	Tapestry No.22/24
◆ Very Fine (#4) Braid	Tapestry No.24/26
◆ Blending Filament	Tapestry No.22/24/26/28
◆ Cord	Tapestry No.24/26/28
◆ Cable	Tapestry No.24/26/28
◆ Japan #1	Tapestry No.24/26/28
◆ Japan #5	Tapestry No.22/20 – couched
◆ Japan #7	Tapestry No.22/20 – couched
◆ Ombre	Tapestry No.22/24

CONTROLLING THREADS

A laying tool can be very useful when you are working with metallic threads to create a smooth, reflective surface. It is also useful when stitching with stranded silk or cotton, for laying metallic ribbons and when top stitching with Hi-Lustre, Glow-in-the-Dark and Vintage Blending Filaments. Using a laying tool keeps multiple strands of thread parallel and separate during the actual stitching process. Properly laid threads reflect the maximum amount of light and give a uniform appearance as seen in the Romance Sampler detail below. Laying tools include a bodkin, teko-bari, trolley needle and a bent weaver's needle.

Thread control is also made easier by dampening some threads, such as Braids, with a cosmetic-type sponge before use, as this will help prevent twisting and knotting. Allowing the needle and thread to drop and spin every so often will help the threads to lie untwisted.

CHOOSING FABRIC FOR METALLIC THREADS

Metallic threads are wonderfully versatile and can be used on any fabric – for counted thread work and all freestyle embroidery. The choice of fabric used will depend on the end use of the design, the type of embroidery being worked and the personal preferences of the stitcher. The fabrics used in this book include blockweave fabrics such as Aida, evenweaves such as linen, canvas and plastic canvas. There is also advice on working on painted (pre-printed) canvas – an increasingly popular medium for use with metallic threads.

BLOCKWEAVES

These fabrics are commonly given the general name of Aida and are woven in bundles or blocks which makes counting easy, as the stitches are formed using these holes. Aidas are made predominantly of cotton and cotton mixes and the fabric is very popular for cross stitch embroidery, with one cross stitch usually worked over one block. The fabric is available from various manufacturers in many colours and counts, the count being the number of blocks per 1in (2.5cm). Using metallic threads on Aida produces beautiful results, as seen by the ethereal effect created on 14 count Aida in Dragonfly Illusion on page 64.

EVENWEAVES

This is the name given to a range of fabrics where the threads are woven singly rather than in blocks, so that there is the same number of threads per 1in (2.5cm) vertically and horizontally. Evenweaves (which include linens) come in a wide variety of thread counts, for example, a 28 count fabric has 28 threads to 1in (2.5cm). Stitching on evenweave is usually done over two threads

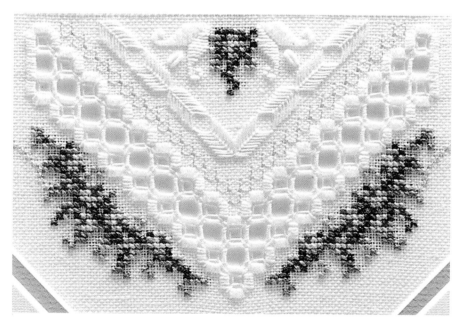

of the fabric, so on a 28 count this will produce 14 stitches to 1in (2.5cm), therefore a design worked on 28 count even-weave will be the same size as when stitched on 14 count Aida (see the stitched butterflies on page 34). As with Aida, evenweaves are available in many colours and counts. The beautifully detailed blackwork of Rhapsody of Lace (page 56) uses a 28 count evenweave, stitched with a range of metallic threads to create various pattern densities.

PLASTIC CANVAS

This is a mesh made from moulded plastic used for counted thread work and ideal for three-dimensional work or embroidery projects requiring more rigidity. It is available in sheets in various counts, though not as wide a range as Aida and evenweave. It is also available in circles. The plastic canvas should be cut to the specified size between the bars, counting bars not holes and trimming off the spikes before stitching. The delightful Celestial Mobile on page 106 (see picture detail below) shows what unusual effects can be achieved by working Glow-in-the-Dark threads on plastic canvas. Refer also to the Plastic Canvas Thread Guide on page 123.

CANVAS

The general style of canvas embroidery we know today (often called needlepoint in the United States) dates back to the sixteenth century in England and France and has remained popular. This popularity today is due in large

part to the easy availability of exciting threads in wide colour ranges which have a variety of textures. Many of the same stitches used for blockweave and evenweave fabrics are also used for canvas embroidery, particularly tent stitch and cross stitch. In Britain, canvas mesh sizes are often measured in holes per inch but using a 'count' number is also a familiar way for most stitchers to identify canvas sizes. Canvas fabrics are made by various manufacturers and counts vary from 3 to 30.

Canvas is usually made of a stiffened cotton but can also be made of silk, linen or synthetic fibres. There are three main types of canvas:

♦ Mono or single – where the warp and weft threads alternate in lying over and under one another.
♦ Interlock – where two thinner vertical threads are twisted around a thicker horizontal one to produce a more stable mesh.
♦ Double or Penelope – which is made up of pairs of vertical and horizontal threads, providing a strong mesh and allowing the stitcher to use every hole, for fine stitching.

Stitching on blank canvas is called counted canvas, and is usually done by following a separately printed stitch diagram or chart. The sumptuous Classic Golden Balantine (page 84 and see picture detail below) is stitched in bands of metallic threads and Silk Mori® on an 18 count mono canvas. For best results when stitching on canvas, mount canvas on stretcher bars or a scroll frame to minimise distortion. Because canvas is abrasive, always use relatively short lengths of thread to minimise friction, and tape or turn under the edges of the canvas.

PAINTED CANVAS

Painted canvas is an exciting, contemporary medium for using metallic threads. Stitching on painted canvas means following a design already painted or printed on the canvas, and over the past fifteen years, Kreinik Braids and Ribbons have been increasingly used to enhance the appearance of painted canvas embroideries by creating dimensional and textural contrast.

In recent years, a greater focus on creating texture and contrast in embroidery has emerged, not only by increasing the use of Kreinik Metallic Threads and Silks, but also by using a greater diversity of stitches. The two trends in unison offer unlimited opportunities to embellish and personalise canvas embroidery designs.

You could also adapt the canvas designs in this book, for example using different thread colours in the Friendship Angel or the Regency Stocking (a detail of which is shown here).

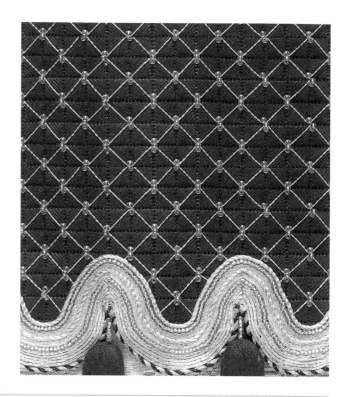

ADAPTING PAINTED CANVASES

Any commercially produced painted (pre-printed) canvas embroidery design can be enhanced or adapted by the use of Kreinik Metallic Threads. The broad range of thread type and colour guarantees the stitcher the ability to express individual creativity and turn a commercial product into a personalised work of art.
Here are a few suggestions:

♦ Try adding simple reflective highlights to realistic themes, using, for example, Blending Filament.

♦ Use Blending Filament throughout geometric designs, or use Braids or Ribbons in specific areas of geometric designs to provide a shimmering contrast to wool or silk.

♦ Work the design as provided on the painted canvas but add subtle Blending Filament to some or all of the plain threads.

♦ Select one or two colours worked in plain thread and replace them completely with metallic threads.

♦ Use metallic threads to outline a design, to visually 'lift' the design elements.

♦ Use metallic threads to create more drama in a border.

♦ Work metallic threads as a shadow line on areas of lettering to give the words more sparkle and emphasis.

♦ Try stitching a painted canvas in plain threads, then use metallic threads over the top of sections of the design, for example, whipping areas of backstitch.

Painted Canvas Kimono Design
(Designed by Lee's Needlearts)

The painted canvas design shown here is an example of how you can explore the use of metallic threads. Examine the design and reflect on your interpretation of it, asking yourself which threads and stitches could be used, and where. The use of different threads and stitches will make the details of a painted canvas come alive with texture, colour and dimension.

This kimono design is enhanced by the use of Kreinik silk and metallic threads. While the backdrop for the clouds and waves has been stitched in simple basketweave stitch using Kreinik Silk Mori®, the remainder of the canvas has been completed using a variety of other techniques and stitches. The cloud shapes are defined and highlighted by couching gold Tapestry (#12) Braid with #1 Japan Gold. Delicate French knots in the gold Braid scatter reflective highlights across the shoulders of the kimono. The crane is stitched in cream Silk Mori® with long and short stitches, replicating the texture of feathers. Using these different threads in this design results in a piece that is more exciting and more enticing to look at.

WORKING THE PROJECTS

The beautiful projects in Chapter 4 contain all the directions needed to complete the pieces, including a full list of the supplies you will need, stitching notes, stepped instructions and any diagrams and charts required.

Before beginning any embroidery project there are certain practical considerations that need to be borne in mind and this short section is a quick reminder, giving basic advice on preparing your fabric for stitching, using hoops and frames, beginning the embroidery in the correct way, and completing your work.

PREPARING FABRIC FOR WORK

You will find stitching much easier if you take a little time to prepare your fabric before you start. You may need to iron embroidery fabrics if they are excessively creased. To prevent fraying whilst stitching, trim the edges of Aida fabric with pinking shears and for evenweaves overcast the edges either by hand or with zigzag stitching by machine. It is also most useful to tape the edges of canvas pieces you are working on to prevent threads from snagging on the abrasive edges.

Finding the centre of the fabric   It is preferable to work counted designs like cross stitch from the centre of the

---

STITCHING TIPS

♦ Always read thread instructions carefully before beginning to stitch.

♦ When removing Cords, Braids, and Ribbons from the spool, you can remove any spiral by running the threads over a slightly dampened cosmetic-quality sponge.

♦ Separate and reassemble multiple strands of silk or stranded cotton (floss) before stitching so they will be parallel and untwisted.

♦ In dry climates, pull the strands of Silk Mori® over a slightly dampened sponge and allow to dry before stitching. This allows you to gain more control over the silk.

♦ It pays to practise unfamiliar stitches on a small scrap of fabric or canvas first before working on the actual embroidery.

♦ Use a needle large enough to open the hole in the fabric or canvas sufficiently but without causing lasting distortion. This will allow the needle and thread to pass through the ground fabric more easily and in turn will reduce thread friction and fraying.

♦ Use a short length of thread, about 45cm (18in) or less, to avoid excessive abrasion when pulling the thread through the fabric or canvas.

♦ When stitching, allow the needle to hang free frequently, or give it a few counter-twists, so the thread can untwist. The way a needle is twisted in stitching, combined with the twist of the threads, often leads to frustrating knots.

♦ Stitch using the 'stab' method, working your stitches in two movements: up vertically, then down vertically through the canvas or fabric.

♦ Keep the wrong side of the embroidery as neat as possible. Avoid travelling from one area to another behind unworked areas of canvas or fabric because the thread may show through on the front. For the same reason trim all thread tails closely.

♦ Use a laying tool (see Glossary, page 124) when stitching with stranded silk or cotton to create the smoothest, most reflective surface.

design outwards (unless otherwise instructed), as this will ensure that the stitching is always central and there is an adequate margin for stretching and framing. To find the centre of the fabric fold it in half and then into quarters. Lightly crease these folds and then mark the central lines with tacking (basting) stitches, which are removed when the work is complete. Match the central square on the chart with the central point on the fabric.

USING HOOPS AND FRAMES

You may like to use a hoop or frame to house your stitching while working, although they are not essential, except perhaps in canvas work. There are many different types available, so find one you are comfortable with, and use one large enough to hold the complete design so your stitches do not get squashed. The advantage of using a hoop or frame means that the fabric remains taut, making control of tension easier. Before starting work, bind the edges of hoops with bias binding to prevent slippage and use tissue paper between the frames to prevent damage to the stitching. Remove the fabric from the hoop each time you finish working to avoid excessive crease marks. Canvas should be mounted on stretcher bars, pulling it drum tight.

STARTING OFF

Starting and finishing thread should be done as neatly as possible to avoid ugly lumps and bumps on your finished embroidery. There are two main ways to begin stitching, as follows.

Using an 'away' waste knot This is made by knotting the end of the thread and placing it on the surface in an area away from where you are stitching. After the stitching is complete, clip the knot from the surface and weave the end of the thread into several stitches on the back of the embroidery, being careful not to disturb the stitches on the surface.

Using an 'in-line' waste knot This is made by knotting the end of the thread and placing it on the surface in line with the first few stitches which will cover the beginning of the thread on the back of the embroidery. Stitch in the direction of the knot and clip it off as you reach it.

COMPLETING PROJECTS

As you can see by the gorgeous projects in this book, metallic threads have endless uses in fine embroidery and the designs created can be displayed in an exciting variety of ways. Some are mounted in pictures, others are displayed in commercial products, of which there is a wide selection on the market today. Other designs are made up into items such as sachets, table linen and cushions.

Stretching and mounting Small projects will not require stretching and if they need to be mounted onto board prior to framing, can simply be attached using double-sided adhesive tape, or sewn on. Larger pieces of work may need more time and effort and will definitely benefit by being taken to a professional picture framer. Canvas projects may need stretching or blocking if the canvas has become distorted during stitching.

Framing Many attractive frames and mounts are available today and can greatly enhance the finished appearance of a design. You may have stitched a design specifically to fit a frame you already have, or you may feel able to do the framing yourself, but in most cases it pays to take your work to a professional framer.

CARING FOR METALLIC THREAD EMBROIDERY

Blending Filaments, Cords, Cables, Braids and Ribbons can be hand-washed, machine-washed or dry-cleaned. Ombre is hand-washable or dry-cleanable. Japan threads can be hand-washed in cold water or dry-cleaned. Facets™ should only be dry-cleaned. Never use bleach on any metallic threads. Blending Filaments, Cords, Cables, Braids, Ribbons and Japan Threads can all be tumble-dried on a low setting. When ironing a finished piece containing metallic threads, do not iron directly on the threads: use a pressing cloth and light or minimum pressure. Do not use steam.

Unlike real metal threads, which should be stored in acid-free tissue paper, metallic threads require no special storage considerations.

chapter 3

STITCHES

THERE ARE A WEALTH OF STITCHES PERFECT FOR USE WITH METALLIC THREADS AND THIS CHAPTER CONTAINS DESCRIPTIONS AND DIAGRAMS OF THE STITCHES USED IN THE DESIGNS IN CHAPTER 4. MANY OF THEM YOU WILL ALREADY BE FAMILIAR WITH, OTHERS ARE INTERESTING VARIATIONS FOR YOU TO TRY. (SEE ALSO RECOMMENDATIONS FOR REFERENCE BOOKS LISTED ON PAGE 125.)

THIS CHAPTER ALSO DESCRIBES HOW TO USE THE CHARTS AND STITCH DIAGRAMS CONTAINED IN THE PROJECTS. FOR THOSE OF YOU WISHING TO WORK THE PROJECTS ON FABRICS AND COUNTS OTHER THAN THOSE QUOTED IN THE DESIGNS, THERE IS A REMINDER ON CALCULATING DESIGN SIZES.

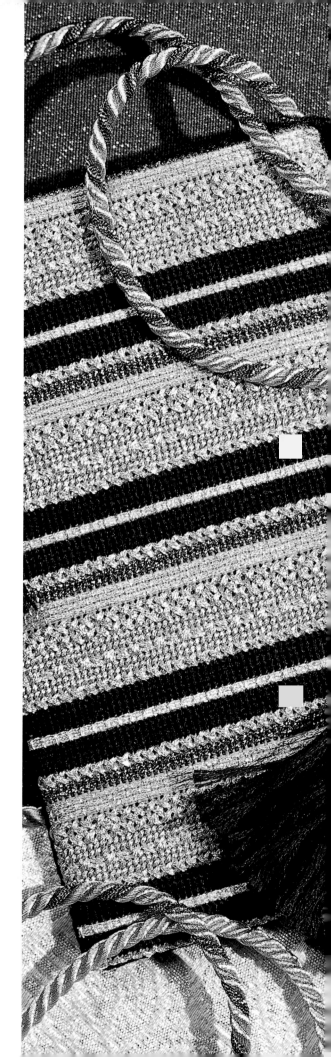

WORKING WITH CHARTS AND STITCH DIAGRAMS

THE CHARTS AND STITCH DIAGRAMS in this book are graphic illustrations that accompany the written project instructions. It is important to understand their differences in order to interpret the instructions correctly.

CHARTS

Fig 5 below depicts a basic chart generally used to indicate colour and stitch placement in a design. Each symbol on the chart represents one stitch, and here there are two different colours represented by the symbols x and o. Project instructions indicate whether each stitch (symbol) is to be executed over one or two fabric threads. Charts split over two pages have no overlap and may be photocopied.

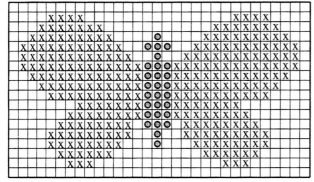

Fig 5 A charted butterfly

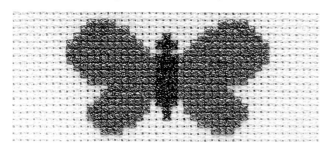

Butterfly cross stitched on 14 count Aida over one block

Butterfly cross stitched on 28-count linen over two threads

STITCH DIAGRAMS

The stitch diagram butterfly (Fig 6) is an illustration showing the same information as in Fig 5 but displayed as the stitches would appear if they were worked in tent stitch on canvas or fabric. Each line on the diagram represents one canvas thread. The two different colours are represented by the light and the dark stitches.

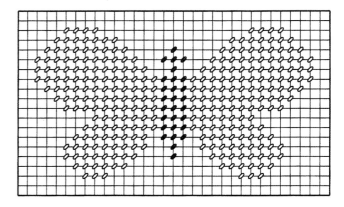

Fig 6 A stitch diagram butterfly

Butterfly tent stitched on 18 count canvas

Butterfly tent stitched on 10 count plastic canvas

STITCH DIAGRAM AND CHART ABBREVIATIONS

The stitch diagrams and charts identifying the colour threads shown within the projects generally use the abbreviations shown below. All designs use only one reel or skein of colour, unless otherwise stated.

BF	Blending Filament
VF	Very Fine (#4) Braid
FN	Fine (#8) Braid
TP	Tapestry (#12) Braid
MD	Medium (#16) Braid
HY	Heavy (#32) Braid
⅛	⅛" Ribbon
¹⁄₁₆	¹⁄₁₆" Ribbon
*	denotes colour availability

CALCULATING DESIGN SIZE

Calculating the design size is necessary when deciding how much fabric you will need to stitch a particular project or whether a particular motif will fit into the picture or card aperture you have chosen. The projects in the book contain stitch count and design size information but if you wish, the projects can be stitched on different fabric counts to the ones given. The finished design size is easily calculated. All that determines the size of a cross stitch design is the number of stitches up and down and the thread count of the fabric. To calculate the size of a design, count the number of stitches horizontally and vertically on the chart. Divide each of these numbers by the number of stitches to 1in (2.5cm) on your fabric (i.e., the count) and this will give you the finished design size.

For example: a design to be worked on a 14 count Aida which is 140 stitches deep on the chart x 56 stitches wide, will, when stitched, be 10in (25cm) deep x 4in (10cm) wide, i.e., 140 ÷ 14 = 10, and 56 ÷ 14 = 4.

You will need to add extra fabric all round to the basic calculation, to allow a margin for working the design and for final mounting.

THE STITCHES

The following instructions and diagrams illustrate how to work the stitches contained in the projects in the book: they are presented alphabetically for easy reference. Some diagrams are numbered for your convenience, indicating the needle comes to the surface of the embroidery at the odd numbers and to the back of the work on the even numbers. Some of the diagrams omit the even numbers in favour of arrows indicating the direction of the stitches.

ALTERNATING MOSAIC STITCH

This stitch creates an interesting variation in pattern by alternating the direction of each unit of three stitches.

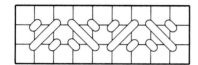

Alternating mosaic stitch

BACKSTITCH

Backstitch is useful for outlining motifs and for placing fine lines in designs. Use a fine thread such as Cord or Very Fine (#4) Braid to backstitch next to other threads. This will create a clean, well-defined outline.

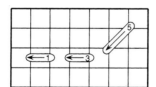

Backstitch

BASKETWEAVE STITCH

Basketweave stitch is worked in diagonal rows. Each stitch is worked over one intersection. The key to working this stitch correctly is to remember to travel *up* the horizontal canvas thread rows and *down* the vertical thread rows. Bring the thread up in an empty canvas hole and go down in a filled hole. End thread tails by sliding under stitching either horizontally or vertically, never diagonally.

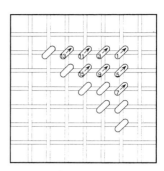

Basketweave stitch

BRICK STITCH

Brick stitch may be used horizontally to create many different stitched effects.

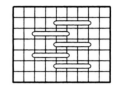

Brick stitch over four threads

BULLION KNOT

Follow a–d in the diagram below for working a bullion knot. Come up at 1 and go down at 2, leaving a loop. Come up at 1 again and wrap the loop around the needle enough times to cover the space between 1 and 2. Hold the wraps and pull the needle and thread through them. Adjust the wraps while going down at 2 to finish the knot.

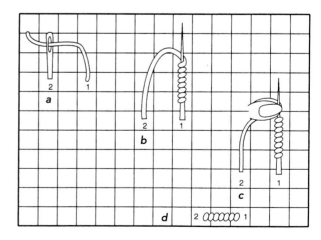

Bullion knot

CORNER DOVE'S EYE STITCH

Corner dove's eye is worked by completing wrapped bars (see page 43) then stitching from corner to corner as shown in the diagram.

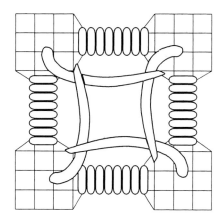

Corner dove's eye stitch

COUCHING

Couching, simply defined, is a method of holding down a line of thread or other material with another thread. It is a linear technique traditionally used to fill solid areas, cover the edges of appliqués and define outlines. Couching may form open fillings, add interest and texture to the background, or become an integral part of a design. Whole areas may be filled with couched threads, which lie so closely together that no canvas or fabric is visible between the threads.

Couching is a technique that adapts well to canvas, especially for use with metallic threads, producing straight or fluid curved lines used either as outlines or areas of solid filling. The diagram below illustrates a few basic techniques of couching threads to the surface of an embroidery. Usually the couching thread will go into the holes of the evenweave fabric or canvas.

Beginning and ending couched threads Allow at least 2.5cm (1in) extra on each end of the working thread. To 'plunge' or take the tail to the reverse side of the fabric or canvas, insert a large eye chenille or tapestry needle (No.18 or 20) halfway into the canvas hole and insert a single strand of the couched thread into the eye of the needle, leaving a small loop. Gently ease each tail through to the reverse side, keeping one hand on the front of the work to gently hold the couched line in place. Anchor the thread securely on the reverse side using small tacking stitches for about 1.25–2cm (½–¾in). Cut off the excess.

Torsades and Facets™ are plunged in much the same manner. Because of their thickness, it is helpful to slightly fan the ends to make threading the eye of the needle easier. Enlarging the canvas hole with an awl or a large tapestry or rug needle prior to plunging also helps to ease the Torsades or Facets™ to the reverse side. Once the tail has been pulled through to the reverse side, give it a slight twist to realign any threads that may have become untwisted on the right side.

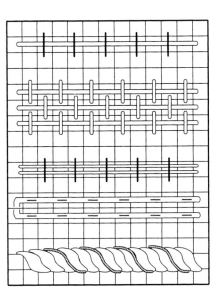

Couching

a A single line of couching with the couched, or laid, thread falling between the lines of fabric or canvas. The laid thread is positioned and secured with the small vertical couching stitches

b This shows multiple rows of couched threads, each one laying in a separate 'valley' of the fabric or canvas

c Here, two rows of couched thread are positioned in the same 'valley' of the fabric or canvas and secured with the same vertical stitch. (This is a traditional approach to couching Japan threads.)

d The couched thread here is held in place by small horizontal stitches which pierce the couched thread. This method is particularly useful for Braids and Ribbons

e A heavily twisted thread may be secured with couching stitches which lay between the twists – a method very useful for twisted cords and Torsades

CROSS STITCH

There are two main ways to make a cross stitch; as an individual whole cross stitch, or in rows in two separate journeys. The diagrams below show both methods.

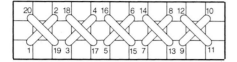

Cross stitch worked singly

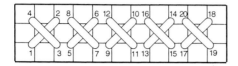

Cross stitch worked in rows

CUSHION ON LINEN STITCH

This stitch provides a padded, square unit. Stitch the units moving left to right across the design area. See also page 72.

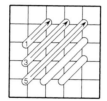

Cushion on linen stitch

DIAGONAL DARNING

Diagonal darning provides a light, open stitch useful for backgrounds or filling in areas. The thread running from one stitch to the next creates a shadow on the front which becomes part of the pattern. It is best to begin and end threads outside the design area so as not to interrupt the pattern.

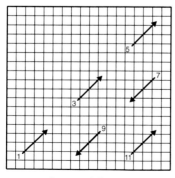

Diagonal darning

DOUBLE BRICK STITCH

Double brick stitches worked in pairs, may be worked straight across the rows, with the alternating units filled in on the return journey.

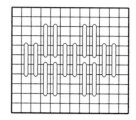

Double brick stitch

FRENCH KNOT

French knots are useful accompaniments to cross stitch, providing accents and texture. Hold the thread in front of the needle and wrap once or twice before going back into the ground fabric or canvas. Reinsert the needle one canvas or fabric thread away from where the needle originally emerged – practising the stitch a few times will show you where best to reinsert the needle.

French knot

HALF CROSS STITCH

Half cross stitch is worked by using a single stitch which slants diagonally from lower left to upper right.

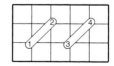

Half cross stitch (over two)

Half cross stitch (over one)

HORIZONTAL GOBELIN STITCH

This stitch may be worked by stitching the rows vertically up and down the canvas.

Horizontal gobelin stitch

HUNGARIAN DIAMOND STITCH

Hungarian diamonds should be worked by completing one unit of five stitches before moving horizontally to stitch the next unit.

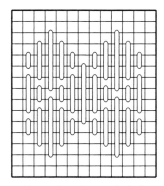

Hungarian diamond stitch

KLOSTER BLOCKS

Kloster blocks are groups of five satin stitches worked over four fabric threads. The stitches at the corners share holes at their bases. Be careful not to carry a thread diagonally across a corner.

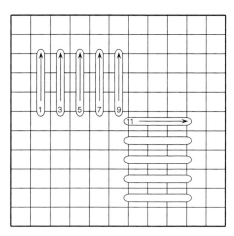

Kloster blocks

LAZY DAISY STITCH

This stitch is often used for ribbon embroidery and is also called detached chain stitch. Come up at 1 and down at 2, holding the thread in a loop. Take a small stitch at 3–4 to secure the stitch in the desired location.

Lazy daisy stitch

LONG AND SHORT STITCH

This produces a realistic, shaded effect, and is useful for filling in fins, leaves and petals – see picture detail below from Poppies, Snails and Peacocks' Tails. The second row of stitches (shown in black) splits the preceding stitches.

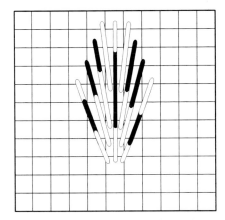

Long and short stitch

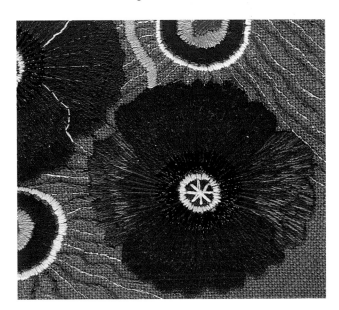

LEAF VARIATION STITCH

This stitch creates the illusion of random leaves. Stitch each leaf individually, taking special care to secure the beginning and ending tails. Do not travel from one leaf to another.

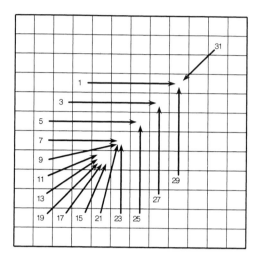

Leaf variation stitch

MERRILYN'S BOW

This is a composite stitch, formed with two horizontal lazy daisy stitches, connected with one cross stitch above two straight stitches which have a slight twist.

Merrilyn's bow

OLD-FASHIONED HEMSTITCH

Old-fashioned hemstitch is frequently used as a decorative stitch, but it was also used years ago for hemming. Work from right to left across your piece.

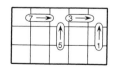

Old-fashioned hemstitch

OUTLINE STITCH

Outline stitch may be worked in any direction, but is shown here moving from left to right while holding the working thread above the line of stitching.

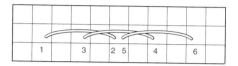

Outline stitch

PARISIAN STITCH

Parisian stitch may be stitched moving either right or left across your work

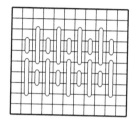

Parisian stitch

PEKINESE STITCH

This stitch is worked by completing a line of backstitches then looping another thread through them on the surface without going to the back of the work.

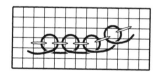

Pekinese stitch

QUEEN STITCH

Queen Stitch creates an elegant textured effect. All vertical stitches begin and end in the same hole and each is tacked down to a vertical fabric thread with a short horizontal stitch. It is better to alternate stitching the vertical stitches by placing the one farthest to the right first, then the one farthest to the left, then the next to the farthest on the right, and so on until the stitch is complete. By carefully using this progression you will create a symmetrical and even stitch.

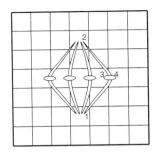

Queen stitch

RIBBON STITCH

This stitch is useful in ribbon embroidery. Come up at 1 and pierce the ribbon at 2. Pull the needle to the back gently and allow the edges of the ribbon to curl at the tip.

Ribbon stitch

REVERSE HALF CROSS STITCH

Reverse half cross stitch is worked by using a single stitch which slants diagonally from lower right to upper left. It may be worked over one or two threads, as shown below.

Reverse half cross stitch (over two)

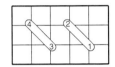

Reverse half cross stitch (over one)

RICE STITCH

Rice stitch is a large cross stitch with each of the 'arms' crossed by smaller stitches, frequently in a different thread and/or colour. It may be executed by stitching the large cross stitches then returning to insert the smaller stitches on a separate journey.

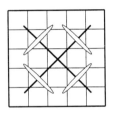

Rice stitch

RHODES STITCH VARIATION

Rhodes stitch variation can be used effectively for snowflakes. Stitch each snowflake individually, taking special care to secure the beginning and ending tails. Do not travel from one snowflake to another.

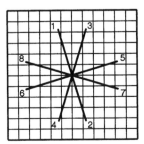

Rhodes stitch variation

RUNNING STITCH EMBELLISHMENT

Running stitch embellishment is a series of short stitches over two canvas threads which further defines the pattern created by blocks of Scotch stitches (see page 42). Complete the slanted Scotch stitches first then work the straight stitches in a series of horizontal then vertical rows.

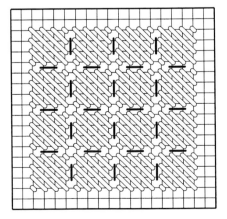

Running stitch embellishment

SATIN STITCH VARIATIONS

Satin stitches are used to form various motifs (see the Romance Sampler detail below). As shown by the diagrams below , they can be used to create many shapes.

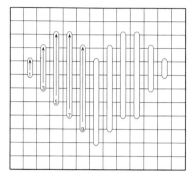

Satin stitch – used to form heart motifs

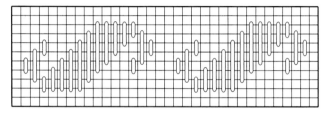

Satin stitch – worked vertically to create scrolls

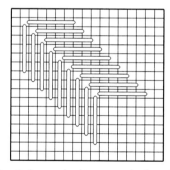

Satin stitch – worked to create leaf motifs

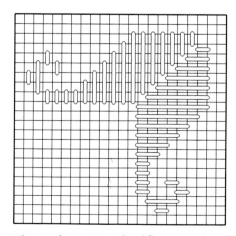

Satin stitch – used to create stylised flowers, such as tulips

SCOTCH STITCH

Units of Scotch stitch form squares which may be alternated with a different colour to create a unique pattern (see the Friendship Angel, page 101).

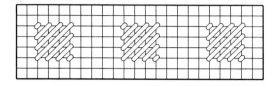

Scotch stitch

SPIDER'S WEB STITCH

The spider's web is useful for flowers. Stitch the spokes first with all stitches sharing the centre hole. Then weave around the shape by going over two spokes and back under one spoke, keeping the thread on the surface of the canvas. Pack the weaving stitches tightly until no more will fit under the spokes, then take the thread to the back of the work and secure the end.

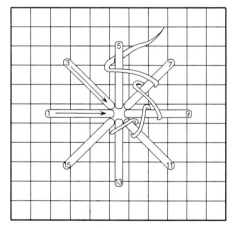

Spider's web stitch

TENT STITCH

Tent stitches are slanted from lower left to upper right. They may be stitched in horizontal rows worked from right to left, or in vertical rows worked from top to bottom.

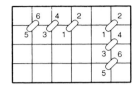

Tent stitch

THREE-QUARTER CROSS STITCH

Three-quarter cross stitches are used to give form and definition around the curves and edges of cross stitch design elements and may be slanted in whatever direction required for that purpose (as shown in the diagram below). They are very easy to work on evenweave; if worked on Aida you will need to pierce the fabric with the quarter stitch.

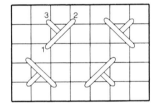

Three-quarter cross stitch

UPRIGHT CROSS STITCH

Also known as upright 2 x 2 stitch. Work each cross in turn. Each stitch covers two threads of the canvas, with the horizontal stitch worked last.

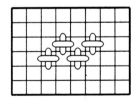

Upright cross stitch

WOVEN STITCH AND WOVEN STITCH VARIATION

These stitches provide attractive filling patterns, as shown by the two diagrams below.

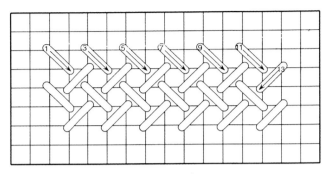

Woven stitch

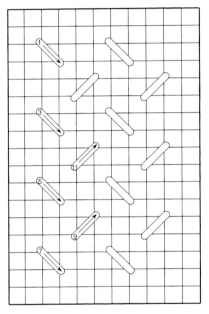

Woven stitch variation

WRAPPED BARS

Loose fabric threads are wrapped together by coming up at 1 and down at 2, keeping the tension uniform and the wraps evenly spaced.

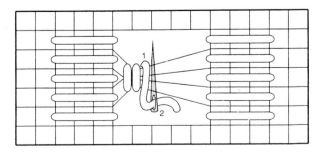

Wrapped bars

chapter 4

c h a p t e r 4

THE DESIGNS

NEVER BEFORE HAS THERE BEEN SUCH AN OUTSTANDING ARRAY OF DESIGNS

SPECIFICALLY PLANNED FOR A BOOK THAT TEACHES HOW TO USE METALLIC

THREADS IN HAND EMBROIDERY. THE PROJECTS THAT FOLLOW HAVE BEEN

DESIGNED AND STITCHED BY LEADING INTERNATIONAL EMBROIDERERS. THESE

TALENTED DESIGNERS WERE SELECTED TO CREATE SCRUMPTIOUS, BEAUTIFUL PRO-

JECTS THAT ENABLE STITCHERS NOT ONLY TO LEARN THE 'HOW', 'WHY', 'WHERE'

AND 'WHEN' OF USING METALLIC THREADS, BUT ALSO TO BECOME FAMILIAR WITH

THE PLANNING PROCESS OF USING THESE ILLUMINATING THREADS.

THESE DESIGNS WERE PLANNED TO SHOW HOW EASY IT IS TO USE METAL-

LIC THREADS AND HOW THE THREADS CAN CHANGE THE VERY NATURE OF A

DESIGN. YOU CAN EASILY TAKE THE CONCEPTS PRESENTED HERE

AND SEE WHERE TO ADD 'SHIMMERS OF LIGHT', WHERE TO CREATE

'REALISTIC EFFECTS' OR WHEN TO ILLUMINATE DETAILS SO THAT THE DESIGN

COMMUNICATES THE RIGHT FEELING. IT IS THIS 'VISUAL PRESENCE', THIS INHER-

ENT CHARACTERISTIC OF METALLIC THREADS TO CAPTURE AND HOLD THE

LIGHT, THAT MAKES METALLIC THREADS THE MOST IMPORTANT TEXTURAL

COMPONENT OF A DESIGN.

OPEN YOURSELF TO THE CHALLENGE AND WONDER OF USING METALLIC

THREADS. THEY WILL CREATE AN IMPACT ON YOUR STITCHERY FOREVER.

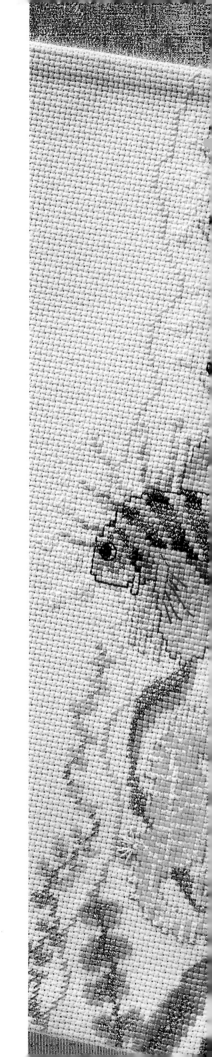

FLIGHT OF NATURE

Designed by Mike Vickery, USA

THE GRACE AND BEAUTY OF THESE HUMMINGBIRDS FLYING TOWARD MORNING GLORIES ARE

REALISTICALLY HIGHLIGHTED AND OUTLINED BY USING KREINIK BLENDING FILAMENT AND CORD.

BLENDING FILAMENT REFLECTS LIGHT, THUS CREATING THE ILLUSION – OR MAGIC – THAT YOU CAN ACTUALLY

'SEE' THE SUNLIGHT ILLUMINATE ELEMENTS OF THE DESIGN, AS SEEN IN THE FLOWER PETALS AND LEAVES.

BLENDING FILAMENT IS ALSO USED TO DEPICT NATURAL EFFECTS, SUCH AS THE IRIDESCENCE OF THE

HUMMINGBIRDS' FEATHERS. KREINIK CORD IS USED IN BACKSTITCHING THE VINES TO OUTLINE AND VISUALLY

LIFT THE DETAILS OFF THE FABRIC, WHICH CREATES A SENSE OF DEPTH. THE CORD HELPS THE EYE

VIEW THE DETAILS OF THE DESIGN AS DISTINCT ENTITIES.

Stitching Notes

Stitch Count: *89 stitches wide x 126 high*
Design Size: *12.75 x 17.75cm (5 x 7in) on 18 count*
Each square on the chart represents one cross stitch.

YOU WILL NEED

♦ 33 x 38cm (13 x 15in) piece of white 18 count Aida
♦ Kreinik Blending Filament: 008 Green, 015 Chartreuse, 025 Grey, 092 Star Pink, 100 White
♦ Kreinik Cord 011C Nickel
♦ Anchor/DMC stranded cotton (floss): 1/White, 46/666, 85/3609, 86/3608, 87/3607, 88/718, 204/913, 205/911, 206/955, 227/701, 230/909, 238/703, 253/472, 256/704, 267/470, 273/645, 390/822, 830/644, 847/3072, 923/699, 1005/816 1029/915, 1040/647, 9046/321

1 Prepare your fabric and begin stitching the design following the chart and key. Use two strands of stranded cotton (floss) for the regular cross stitches.

Use one strand of stranded cotton (floss) and two strands of Kreinik Blending Filament (KBF) blended together in the needle for cross stitches where indicated on the chart key.

2 After all the cross stitching is complete, use one strand of Kreinik Cord 011C Nickel to work the back-stitching.

3 When all stitching is complete your embroidery can be prepared for mounting and framing.

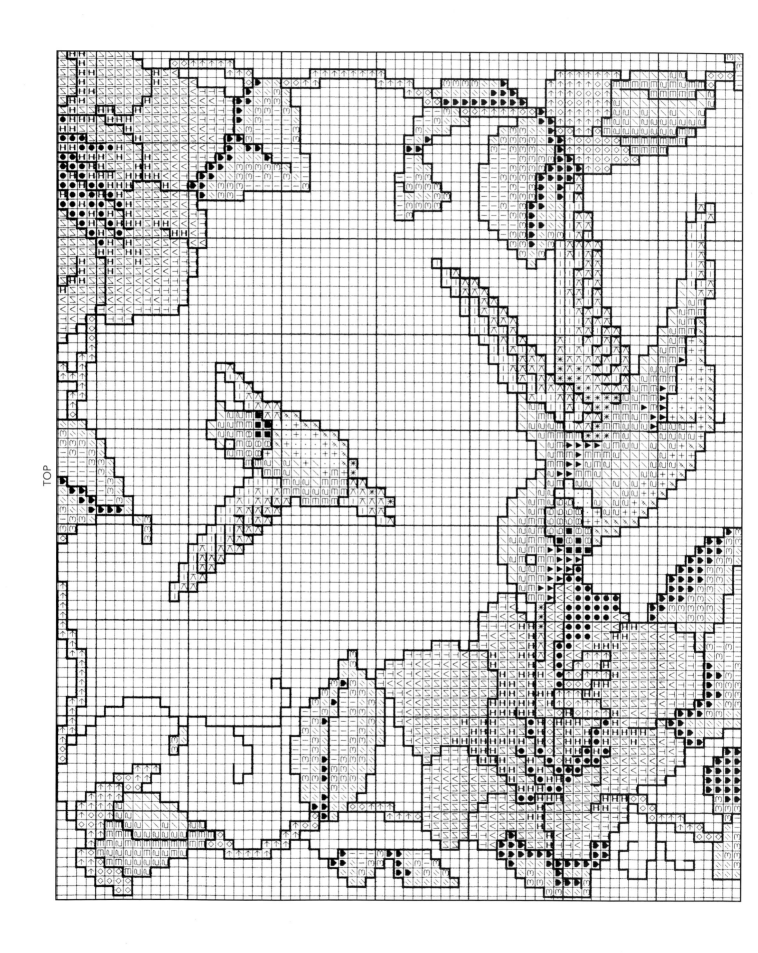

TOP

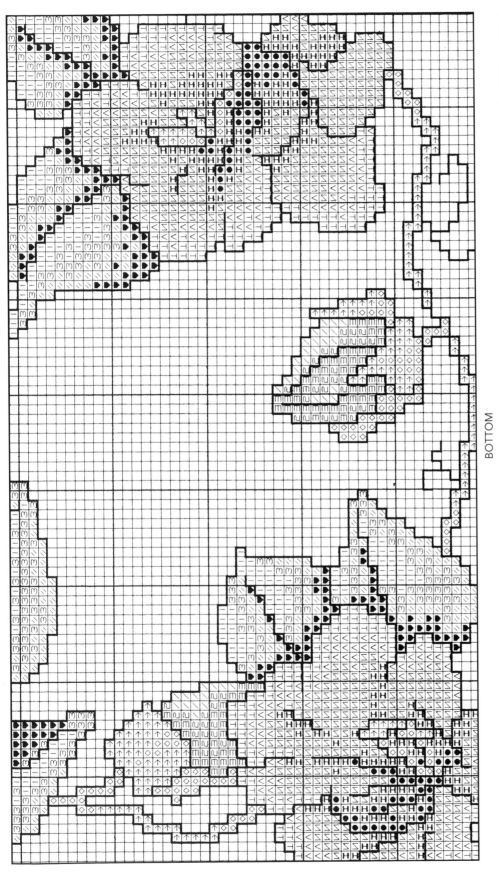

BOTTOM

FLIGHT OF NATURE CHART KEY

	ANCHOR/DMC	KREINIK		ANCHOR/DMC	KREINIK
/	256/704		✳	273/645	
⩔	87/3607		H	88/718	
⟨	86/3608		▶	923/699	
✕	830/644		◗	230/909	
+	390/822		●	1029/915	
T	85/3609	with KBF 092	■	1005/816	
//	205/911				
↑	253/472	with KBF 015		BACKSTITCH WITH	
⊞	227/701		—	KREINIK CORD 011C NICKEL	

	ANCHOR/DMC	KREINIK
●	1/WHITE	
—	847/3072	
⌐	206/955	
2	238/703	with KBF 025
3	204/913	with KBF 100
6	46/666	
8	9046/321	
⋋	1040/647	
◇	267/470	

FANTASY COVE

Designed by Donna Vermillion Giampa, USA

IMAGINE YOURSELF IN SCUBA GEAR BENEATH TRANSPARENT BLUE WATERS OF A COVE, DISCOVERING

NATURE'S SEA LIFE SWIMMING THROUGH GENTLY WAVING SEAWEED. ADDING METALLIC THREADS ENABLES YOU TO

DEPICT NATURE'S SPLENDOUR, CAPTURING THE BRILLIANCE OF COLOUR AND THE TEXTURE OF LIFE FORMS. BY

ADDING THESE TOUCHES OF METALLIC, THE NEEDLEWORK BECOMES MORE REALISTIC AND VISUALLY APPEALING.

THE CONTRAST OF THE METALLIC THREADS TO THE STRANDED COTTON (FLOSS) EMPHASISES THAT NATURE

AND ITS PRECIOUS GIFTS ARE NOT FLAT AND DULL, BUT INHERENTLY DIMENSIONAL AND SPARKLING.

Stitching Notes

Stitch Counts and Finished Sizes:

Placemat: 58 stitches wide x 180 high; 48 x 33cm
(19 x 13in)
Napkin: 43 stitches wide x 71 high; 42 x 42cm
(16½ x 16½in)
Napkin ring: 20 stitches wide x 17 high; 17.75 x 5cm
(7 x 2in)
Mug: 36 stitches wide x 41 high; 26.5 x 9cm
(10½ x 3½in)
Follow the chart key for the number of strands of thread
to use.
Each square on the chart represents one cross stitch and
the design also contains half cross stitches.

YOU WILL NEED

- Light blue 14 count Aida:
  Placemat: two pieces 51 x 35.5cm (20 x 14in)
  Napkin: one piece 42 x 42cm (16½ x 16½in)
  Napkin ring: one piece 20 x 13cm (8 x 5in)
  Mug: one piece 27 x 9cm (10½ x 3½in)
- An acrylic mug with stitching panel (see
  Suppliers, page 126)
- Kreinik Very Fine (#4) Braid: 032 Pearl, 091 Star
  Yellow, 191 Pale Yellow, 052F Grapefruit, 9192 Light

Peach, 094 Star Blue, 194 Pale Blue, 684
Aquamarine, 2122 Curry, 021 Copper, 008 Green,
015 Chartreuse

- Anchor/DMC stranded cotton (floss): 168/807,
  169/806, 170/3765, 185/964, 186/959, 187/958,
  228/700, 235/414, 255/907, 289/307, 290/444,
  302/743, 303/742, 304/741, 323/3825, 324/721,
  324/722, 326/720, 359/801, 361/738, 362/437,
  381/938, 387/739, 398/415, 403/310, 1045/436
- Sewing thread to match fabric

To make the placemat:

1   Prepare one of the pieces of Aida for embroidery –
the 51 x 35.5cm (20 x 14in) size allows for a 1.25cm (½in)
seam allowance plus one empty fabric thread above
and below the design area. The design needs to be
positioned 1.25cm (½in) from the right edge (2.5cm/1in
from the cut edge), with one empty fabric thread left
above and below the design area.

Work the full and half cross stitches in stranded
cotton (floss) and Kreinik Very Fine (#4) Braid as shown
on the chart and described in the key. (The half cross
stitches are shown by a symbol in one half of a chart
square.)

2   Work all the backstitch, as shown on the chart and
described in the key. (Continue on page 55.)

FANTASY COVE CHART KEY

THREADS USED FOR FULL CROSS STITCHES (use 2 strands)

	ANCHOR/DMC or KREINIK BRAID (KVFB)	COLOUR
▪	KVFB 032	Kreinik #4 Braid Pearl
■	403/310	Black
★	290/444	Lemon dark
=	289/307	Lemon
O	KVFB 091	Kreinik #4 Braid Star yellow
H	KVFB 191	Kreinik #4 Braid Pale yellow
ʌ	KVFB 052F	Kreinik #4 Braid Grapefruit
◆	326/720	Orange spice dark
♡	324/721	Orange spice medium
m	324/722	Orange spice light
⟩	323/3825	Pumpkin pale
+	KVFB 9192	Kreinik #4 Braid Light peach
◤	304/741	Tangerine medium
¢	303/742	Tangerine light
−	302/743	Yellow medium
⊓	169/806	Peacock blue dark
◉	168/807	Peacock blue
∅	KVFB 094	Kreinik #4 Braid Star blue
U	KVFB 194	Kreinik #4 Braid Pale blue
⬡	KVFB 684	Kreinik #4 Braid Aquamarine
✚	187/958	Sea green dark
III	186/959	Sea green medium
/	185/964	Sea green light
⤓	398/415	Pearl grey
▨	381/938	Coffee brown ultra dark
✖	KVFB 2122	Kreinik #4 Braid Curry
@	KVFB 021	Kreinik #4 Braid Copper
~	1045/436	Tan
T	362/437	Tan light
⌐	361/738	Tan very light
C	387/739	Tan ultra very light
◿	228/700	Christmas green bright
X	KVFB 008	Kreinik #4 Braid Green
✿	KVFB 015	Kreinik #4 Braid Chartreuse
I	255/907	Parrot green light

THREADS USED FOR HALF CROSS STITCHES (use 1 strand)

	ANCHOR/DMC or KREINIK BRAID (KVFB)	COLOUR
⋔	187/958	Sea green dark
?	186/959	Sea green medium
✧	185/964	Sea green light
◖	228/700	Christmas green bright
⋈	KVFB 008	Kreinik #4 Braid Green
⚲	KVFB 015	Kreinik #4 Braid Chartreuse
⌐	255/907	Parrot green light

THREADS USED FOR BACKSTITCHES (use 1 strand)

	ANCHOR/DMC or KREINIK BRAID (KVFB)	COLOUR/POSITION. (**Note:** all backstitch appears black on the chart)
– – –	KVFB 032	Kreinik #4 Braid Pearl – seahorse's tail lines
——	403/310	Black – eyes
╫╫╫	326/720	Orange spice dark – front yellow fin, inner vein and outline of lionfish, backside of yellow fin outline
╫╫╫	170/3765	Peacock blue very dark – 3 yellow fishes blue part of body outline
——	235/414	Steel grey dark – long straight stitches and outlines of lionfish's tail fin and upper fin
━━	359/801	Coffee brown dark – lionfish's main body outline
– · –	KVFB 2122	Kreinik #4 Braid Curry – vein on lionfish's front fin and seahorse's eye
– ·· –	KVFB 021	Kreinik #4 Braid Copper – large lionfish's main body
—·—	1045/436	Tan – 3 yellow fishes yellow part of body outlines; seahorse; lionfish's fins and fin veins

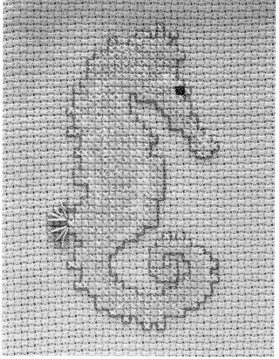

Embellish a greetings card or other small items by simply picking out individual motifs, such as this charming little seahorse

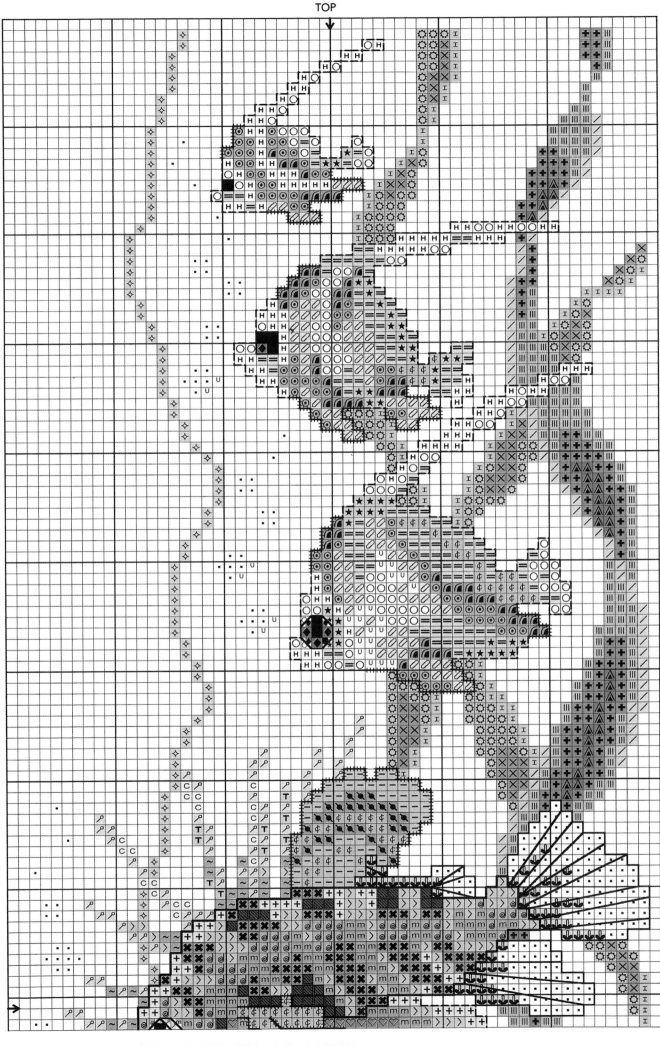

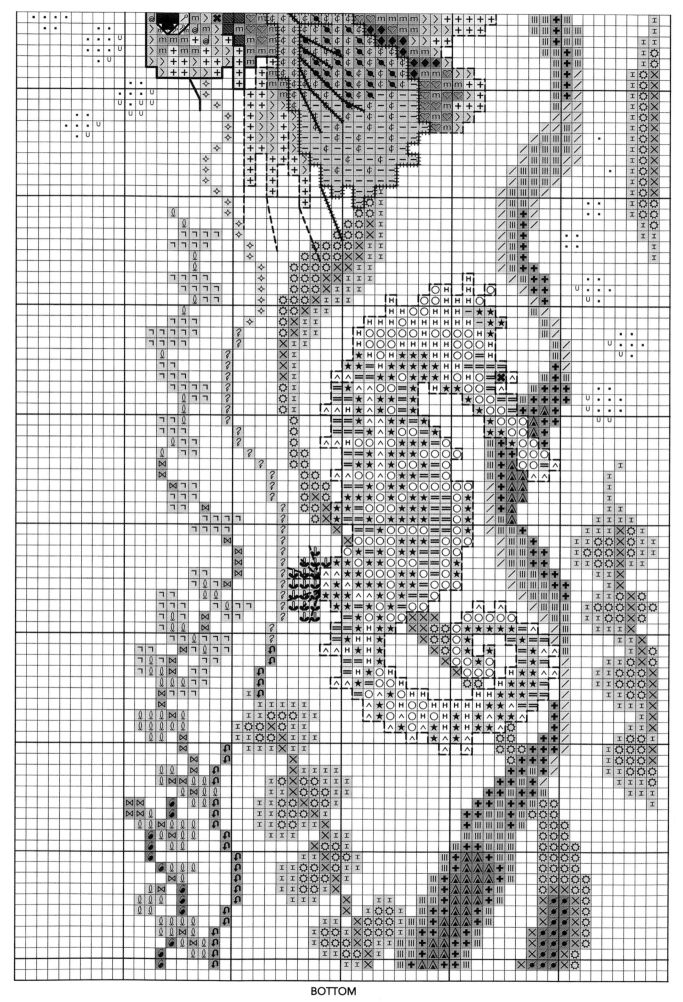

BOTTOM

3 Complete the placemat design by stitching the seahorse in the upper left corner, positioning it about 1.25cm (½in) from the edges.

4 Back the placemat with the second piece of Aida by placing right sides together and stitching all round (leaving a small gap for turning). Turn through to the right side and slipstitch the opening closed.

To make the napkin:

1 Prepare the 42 x 42cm (16½ x 16½in) piece of Aida. Following the chart and key as before, stitch the three fish from the top of the chart along with some of the bubbles and seaweed (see photograph for placement of the motifs).

2 Once the stitching is complete, hand sew or machine stitch a line 2cm (¾in) in from the edge all around and then fringe the edges of the napkin up to this line.

Admire the fish blowing gentle metallic bubbles on the napkin ring and watch them swim past shimmering seaweed on the mug

To make the napkin ring:

1 Prepare the 20 x 13cm (8 x 5in) piece of Aida and stitch the smallest fish and its bubbles in the centre of the fabric.

2 Fold a 1.25cm (½in) seam to the back all round and slipstitch with sewing thread for a finished size of 18 x 5cm (7 x 2in). From the wrong side, slipstitch the two short ends together to form a ring. Turn to the right side.

To make the mug:

1 Prepare the 27 x 9cm (10½ x 3½in) piece of Aida – this allows for a 1.25cm/½in overlap but you may need a different sized piece if your mug is a different one from ours. Stitch the top two fish from the chart along with some of the bubbles and seaweed.

2 Once all the stitching is complete, place the design in the mug so the handle is to the right (if you are right-handed) and the design is positioned approximately in the centre of the straight-on view of the mug.

RHAPSODY OF LACE

Designed by Janelle Giese, USA

BLACKWORK, A CLASSIC EMBROIDERY STYLE USED TO IMITATE LACE, ORIGINATED IN THE FOURTEENTH CENTURY AND BECAME VERY FASHIONABLE IN THE COURT OF HENRY VIII IN ENGLAND IN THE SIXTEENTH CENTURY. THE USE OF METALLIC THREADS IN BLACKWORK TODAY HAS BECOME POPULAR BECAUSE IT OFFERS MORE OPPORTUNITIES TO VARY THE DENSITY AND TONE OF THE PATTERNS WHILE STILL CREATING THE DELICACY NOTED IN FINE LACE.

IN THIS DESIGN FOR A SMALL CUSHION, STITCHES ALTERNATE BETWEEN KREINIK CORD, VERY FINE BRAID AND FINE BRAID TO ACHIEVE VARIOUS PATTERN DENSITIES. A LIGHT DENSITY IS ACHIEVED WITH CORD, A THIN METALLIC, IN AN OPENWORK PATTERN. DARK TONES IN SLIGHTLY THICKER METALLIC THREADS CREATE PATTERNS THAT ARE MORE DENSE. JANELLE GIESE HAS USED A TECHNIQUE TO BUILD DEPTH BY LAYING TWO PARALLEL STRANDS OF FINE BRAID AND USING THEM TO CRADLE A THIRD STRAND OF THINNER VERY FINE BRAID, ALL OF WHICH ARE COUCHED WITH CORD. THE RESULT IS A SUBTLE BUT DEFINITE CHANGE IN HEIGHT (DEPTH), PROVIDING A VISUAL DISTINCTION TO THE STRAIGHT LINE BORDER THAT SEPARATES THE INNER FIELD OF BLACKWORK FROM THE OUTER BORDER. THIS CAN ONLY BE ACHIEVED WITH THREADS THAT CAN CREATE DEPTH, A QUALITY THESE ROUND THREADS POSSESS.

Stitching Notes

Stitch Count: 70 x 70

Design Size: 12.75 x 12.75cm (5 x 5in) on 28 count evenweave

Each square on the chart represents two fabric threads.
Use single strands for the Kreinik threads unless otherwise instructed.

YOU WILL NEED

- Two pieces 28 x 28cm (11 x 11in) of ivory 28 count evenweave fabric
- Kreinik Cord: 201C Chocolate, 215C Antique Copper, 2122 Curry
- Kreinik Very Fine (#4) Braid: 005 Black, 205C Antique Gold, 2122 Curry
- Kreinik Fine (#8) Braid 022 Brown
- Anchor/DMC stranded cotton (floss) 903/3032
- 28 x 28cm (11 x 11in) piece of muslin for lining
- 19 x 19cm (7½ x 7½in) piece of muslin for lining backing fabric
- 90cm (1yd) of trimming
- Polyester filling

1 Prepare the fabric for work, mounting in a frame if desired. Fig 1 on page 58 shows the areas of the design referred to in the instructions. (See picture, page 16.)

To work the central panel:

2 Backstitch the horizontal and vertical grid lines (indicated on the chart by solid black lines) using Cord 201C. Then backstitch the remaining pattern of the panel (indicated in red) using Cord 215C.

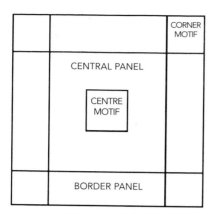

Fig 1   The areas of the design

3   To work the heavy couched lines which form the square around the central panel, the laid thread is a group of three strands of metallic thread. First, lay two strands of Fine (#8) Braid 022 the length indicated on the chart, then add a length of Very Fine (#4) Braid 205C on top. Couch these three strands in place with Cord 201C, making the couching stitches every two fabric threads (see Fig 2). When each side of the square is finished take the lengths of metallic braid to the back and finish off as described on page 37.

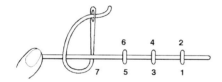

Fig 2   Couching

To work the centre and corner motifs:

4   Begin with the centre motif and, using Very Fine (#4) Braid 005, backstitch the flourishes and centre square (see Fig 3a). Complete each 'arm' individually. The journey of the working thread should return to the centre each time before travelling to the next 'arm' – this is so it does not create a shadow on the front of the work.

Fig 3a

Backstitch the flowerlets (shown in red on the chart) with Very Fine (#4) Braid 2122 Curry following the direction of arrows as indicated in Fig 3b.

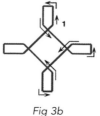

Fig 3b

Now couch the square around the whole motif (Fig 3c). Use Cord 201C for the couching thread and Fine (#8) Braid 022 for the laid thread, spacing the couching thread in one-stitch increments (see step 3). Couch by bringing the laid thread up at the point indicated.

Fig 3c

Work from right to left, continuing to work over the laid thread at the intersections. When complete, bring the laid thread into the fabric at the point where you began and whipstitch the ends to the back using Cord.

To work the border panels:

5   Following the chart, and with reference to the key for the border panels, backstitch the solid black lines shown on the chart with Very Fine (#4) Braid 005. (See photograph on page 16.)

Next, form cross stitches where indicated by the black dots on the chart, using three strands of stranded cotton (floss) Anchor 903 or DMC 3032.

Now, backstitch the individual flowerlets (shown in red on the chart), using Very Fine (#4) Braid 2122.

Work the running stitches (charted with a broken blue line) with one strand of stranded cotton (floss) 903/3032.

To make up the cushion:

6   Begin by pinning the 28cm (11in) square of muslin to the back of the embroidered design and machine stitch the pieces together 3cm (1¼in) beyond the perimeter of the stitched design. Cut the fabric outside the machine-stitched line.

7   Tack (baste) the length of trimming to the right side of the design allowing for a 1.25cm (½in) seam.

8   Take the second piece of evenweave and back it with the 19cm (7½in) square piece of muslin. Pin the front and back, right sides together. Leaving an opening for turning, machine stitch a 1.25cm (½in) seam. Clip the corners and turn to the right side. Stuff with filling, whipstitch the opening closed and hand sew the trim into place.

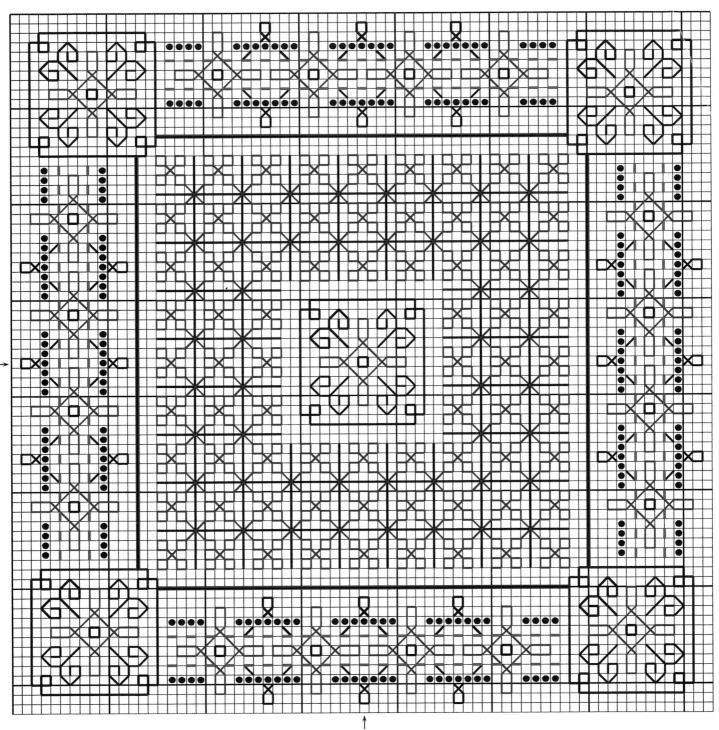

RHAPSODY OF LACE BORDER PANEL CHART KEY

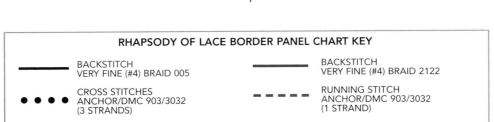

BACKSTITCH
VERY FINE (#4) BRAID 005

BACKSTITCH
VERY FINE (#4) BRAID 2122

CROSS STITCHES
ANCHOR/DMC 903/3032
(3 STRANDS)

RUNNING STITCH
ANCHOR/DMC 903/3032
(1 STRAND)

ANGELIC MESSENGER

Designed by Donna Vermillion Giampa, USA

IT IS SAID THAT ANGELS COME AS THOUGHTS, AS VISIONS, AS DREAMS, AS THE LIGHT IN THE WATER

OR AS CLOUDS AND RAINBOWS. NO MATTER HOW THEY VISIT, WINGED SPIRITS ARE PART OF THE MYSTERY OF

EVERY CULTURE. ANGELS ARE NOTED FOR THEIR WARMTH AND LIGHT; FOR EMITTING AN ETHEREAL RADIANCE THAT

IS ASSOCIATED WITH BRINGING MESSAGES OF HOPE AND GIVING AID AND GUIDANCE. USING BLENDING FILAMENT

TO CREATE THE RADIATING BACKGROUND DRAWS YOUR EYE TO THE ANGELIC POISE. DUE TO THE CONTRAST

BETWEEN THE BACKGROUND AND THE FIGURES, THE ANGEL, WITH THE CUPIDS ACCOMPANYING HER, APPEARS

TO FLOAT IN AIR. THE GENTLE WEAVING OF THE FLOWERED VINE SYMBOLISES THE LOVE, CALM SERENITY

AND GENTLE GUIDANCE THAT SUMMARISES THE CLASSIC DEPICTION OF ANGELS.

YOU WILL NEED

- 30.5 x 35.5cm (12 x 14in) piece of antique white 28 count linen
- Kreinik Blending Filament: 006 Blue, 014 Sky Blue, 032 Pearl, 092 Star Pink, 094 Star Blue
- Kreinik Very Fine (#4) Braid: 002 Gold, 007 Pink, 014 Sky Blue, 102 Vatican Gold
- Kreinik Fine (#8) Braid: 007 Pink, 9200 Blossom
- Anchor/DMC stranded cotton (floss): 1/White, 23/818, 25/3716, 73/963, 75/962, 76/961, 158/747, 167/3766, 168/807, 169/806, 262/3363, 273/3787, 358/433, 361/738, 362/437, 374/420, 381/938, 386/3823, 390/822, 392/642, 778/3774, 830/644, 852/3047, 858/524, 860/522, 862/520, 883/3064, 887/3046, 888/3045, 903/640, 928/3761, 936/632, 944/869, 1008/3773, 1009/3770, 1021/761, 1022/760, 1024/3328, 1037/3756, 1045/436, 1046/435, 4146/950

1   Prepare your fabric and begin stitching the design in full and half cross stitches following the chart and key. (Half cross stitches are shown by a symbol in one half of a chart square.) Use the strands of thread as indicated in the chart key, noting where threads are blended together.

Stitching Notes

Stitch Count: *81 stitches wide x 108 high*

Design Size: *14.5 x 19.5cm (5¾ x 7¾in) on 28 count linen*

Each square on the chart represents one cross stitch, worked over two linen threads (the design also contains half cross stitches).

Follow the chart key for the number of strands of thread to use and where to blend threads.

2   After all the cross stitching is complete, work the backstitches as indicated on the chart. The key gives details of where all the different coloured backstitching occurs.

3   When all stitching is complete your embroidery can be prepared for mounting and framing.

ANGELIC MESSENGER CHART KEY

THREADS USED FOR FULL CROSS STITCHES

	STRANDS	ANCHOR/DMC or KREINIK THREAD	COLOUR
	2	883/3064	Copper medium
	2	1008/3773	Chicory medium
3	2	4146/950	Flesh medium light
□	2	778/3774	Flesh light
/	2	1009/3770	Copper very light
	2	903/640	Tawny medium
	2	392/642	Linen medium
	2	830/644	Sierra very light
C	2	390/822	Linen very light
•	Blend:		
	1	1/White	White with
	1	KBF 032	Pearl
✳	Blend:		
	1	1022/760	Peony medium light with
	1	1021/761	Peony light
●	2	168/807	Surf blue light
✖	2	167/3766	Surf blue very light
	Blend:		
	1	928/3761	Larkspur light with
	1	KBF 094	Star blue
>	2	158/747	Sapphire very light
o	2	1037/3756	Sea blue very light
	2	888/3045	Sand stone medium
♥	2	76/961	Antique rose medium
	2	75/962	Antique rose light
	Blend:		
	1	25/3716	Carnation light with
	1	KBF 092	Star pink
√	2	73/963	Antique rose very light
—	2	23/818	Carnation very very light
◈	2	VFB8 092	Pink
	2	860/522	Laurel green medium light
α	2	858/524	Laurel green light
	2	861/3363	Laurel dark
(	2	386/3823	Citrus very light
⌘	2	374/420	Desert medium dark
S	2	887/3046	Stand stone light
=	2	886/3047	Sand stone
	2	VFB8 002	Gold
	2	1046/435	Toast
	2	1045/436	Light toast
	2	362/437	Nutmeg medium light
△	2	361/738	Nutmeg very light
●	2	VFB8 9200	Blossom
▲	2	VFB4 007	Pink
✖	2	VFB4 102	Vatican gold

THREADS USED FOR HALF CROSS STITCHES

	STRANDS	KREINIK THREAD	COLOUR
	2	KBF 006	Blue
	2	KBF 094	Star Blue
	2	KBF 014	Sky Blue
~	2	KBF 092	Star Pink

THREADS USED FOR BACKSTITCHES (use 1 strand)

	ANCHOR/DMC or KREINIK THREAD	COLOUR/POSITION
——	936/632	Fawn very dark – angel's face, arms, hands; cupids' faces, bodies, arms, hands & feet
- -	273/3787	Stone grey dark – all wings
┼┼┼┼	169/806	Surf blue medium – angel's blue dress, cupid's blue fabric swash
——	76/961	Antique rose medium – angel's pink fabric swash, cupids' pink fabric swashes
——	1024/3328	Peony medium – all mouths
- - -	862/520	Laurel green dark – branches of flowers in centre area and upper right corner
┼┼┼┼	944/869	Wheat dark – angel's & cupid's blonde hair
——	381/938	Fudge dark – eyes
- - -	358/433	Coffee – cupid's brown hair
——	KVFB4 002	Gold – border straight stitches
——	KVFB4 014	Sky blue – inner border backstitch line

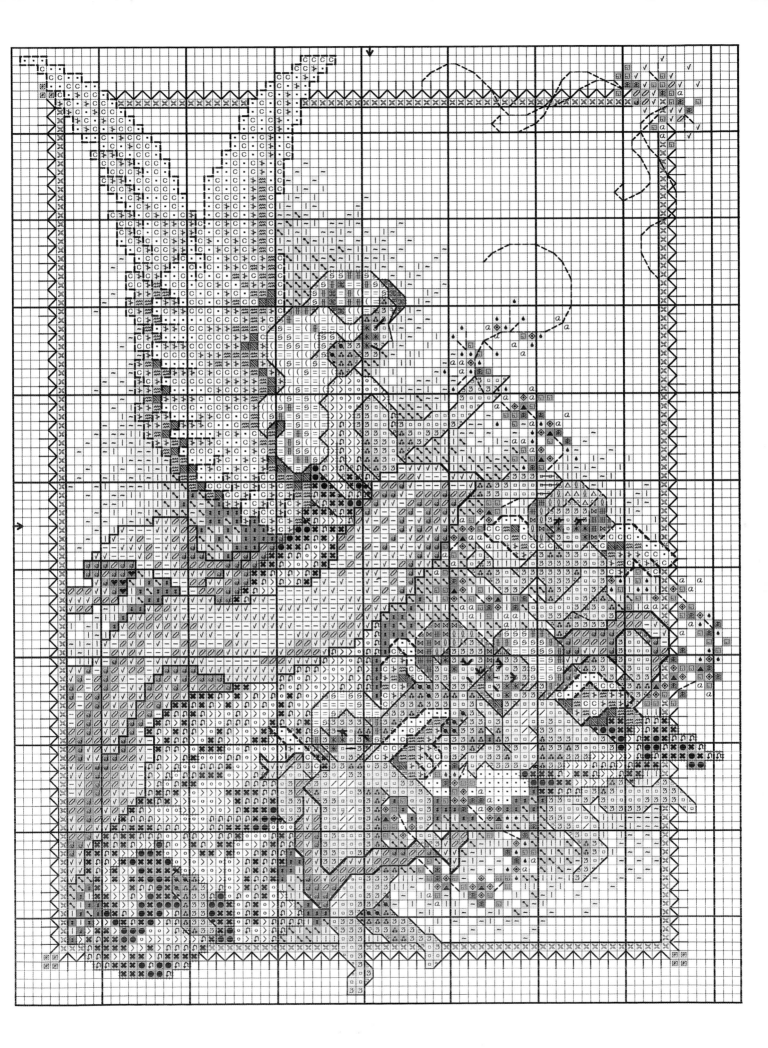

DRAGONFLY ILLUSION

Designed by Janelle Giese, USA

THIS DRAGONFLY FLOATS OVER NATURE'S SUBTLE MIST WITH SILVER, JEWEL-TIPPED WINGS FOR ALL TO

ADMIRE. HALF STITCHES ARE FORMED OVER THE FABRIC USING A SINGLE STRAND OF STRANDED COTTON (FLOSS)

IN PASTEL HUES. A SINGLE STRAND OF WHITE BLENDING FILAMENT IS THEN CROSSED BACK OVER ONE HUE TO

CREATE THE SOFT, SHIMMERY EFFECT OF A WASH OF COLOUR. THIS PRODUCES A VERY DELICATE IMAGERY. KREINIK

JAPAN THREADS ARE COUCHED IN AN OPEN PATTERN TO CREATE WINGS OF HIGH RADIANCE AND SMOOTH

SHEEN WHICH EVOKE THE ILLUSION OF TRANSPARENT GOSSAMER WINGS.

Stitching Notes

Stitch Count: *58 stitches wide x 58 high*
Design Size: *10 x 10cm (4 x 4in) on 14 count*
Each square on the chart represents one fabric block.

YOU WILL NEED

♦ 28 x 28cm (11 x 11in) piece of pale green 14 count Aida
♦ Kreinik Blending Filament 005 Black, 025 Grey, 100 White
♦ Kreinik Very Fine (#4) Braid 001C Silver, 005 Black
♦ Kreinik #1 Japan 001J Silver
♦ Kreinik #5 Japan 001J Silver
♦ Kreinik #7 Japan 001J Silver
♦ Anchor/DMC stranded cotton (floss): 2/White, 69/3743, 232/452, 274/928, 379/840, 403/310, 869/3743, 926/712, 1041/844, 1042/504, 8581/646
♦ Box to house embroidery (see Suppliers, page 126)

1 Prepare the piece of Aida for work and mount it into an embroidery frame if you wish.

To work the background:
2 Work the stitches for the background using the threads listed. Use half cross stitches with one strand of stranded cotton (floss). The X symbol denotes one strand of 1042/504 for the first half of a cross stitch and then one strand of Blending Filament 100 for the second part of the cross stitch.

3 Work the outer border by couching Very Fine (#4) Braid 001C with #1 Japan Silver. Backstitch the inner border with one strand of stranded cotton (floss) 232/452.

To work the dragonfly body:
4 First outline the body in backstitch with one strand of 1041/844. To work the dragonfly's upper body, follow the chart and upper body key and work in the following order: cross stitch, satin stitch, backstitch, straight stitch, and French knot using the threads and amounts listed. (Note: For colour 'fullness' on fractional stitches, place three-quarter cross stitches back to back inside areas of the body.)

5 Now work the dragonfly's padded lower body. This was outlined in backstitch in step 4. The next step is to couch vertical stitches to make the lower body dimensional. The couching is worked in two stages. First, follow the outline shape to lay the vertical threads using three layers of colour. For the first layer, use the full six strands of 379/840 to fill the entire length of the body with vertical stitches. For the second layer (or colour) use three strands of 232/452 to centre vertical stitches on

top of the first layer. For the last layer (or colour) centre three laid stitches of 869/3743 on top of the previous two layers. (See also the picture detail on page 14.)

The final stage is to place straight stitches horizontally over the vertical stitches. Referring to the chart for placement, use one strand of Kreinik Very Fine (#4) Braid 005 Black to lay horizontal threads across the lower body. Notice these threads are placed between the fabric holes (by piercing the fabric) and are pulled up

at the centre when couched. With this in mind, keep tension slightly relaxed when laying these horizontal threads. After all horizontal threads are in place, use two strands of the Black #4 Braid to lay a final vertical length up the centre which will secure the padded lower body (Fig 1). Each stitch should be taken at the centre of normal stitch placement, pulling up the horizontal laid threads to arch as shown on the dragonfly chart (see below and the photographs).

DRAGONFLY CHART

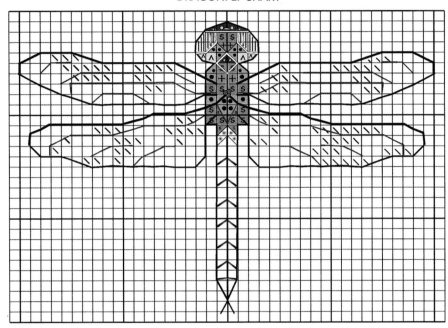

DRAGONFLY ILLUSION CHART KEYS

DRAGONFLY KEY – UPPER BODY

✳	403/310	
Λ	232/452	
S	8581/646	
▪	379/840	
⊡	1041/844	
⊞	869/3743	

│	379/840	Vertical satin stitch, 3 strands fill in for eyes
──	1041/844	Backstitch, 2 strands for eyes, 1 for body
╏	2/White	Straight stitch, 3 strands for eye & nose highlights
‖	8581/646	Straight stitch, 3 strands for vertical line of centre body
V	403/310	Straight stitch, 2 strands for lower back 'V'
❦	379/840	French knots, 3 strands

DRAGONFLY KEY – WINGS

──── Couch upper edges of wings, using Japan Silver for laid thread and 1 strand #1 Japan Silver for couching

──── Backstitch lower outline of wings, 1 strand Blending Filament 005

╲ Half cross stitches on wings, 1 strand Blending Filament 005. Fill in wing area for all unmarked stitches using half cross stitches and 1 strand Blending Filament 025

── ── Couch interior lines of all wings using #5 Japan Silver as laid thread and 1 strand of #1 Japan Silver for couching

BACKGROUND KEY

▪	926/712	Half cross stitch, 1 strand
⑤	69/3743	Half cross stitch, 1 strand
L	274/928	Half cross stitch, 1 strand
⁄	1042/504	Half cross stitch, 1 strand
☒	1042/504 plus KBF100 for second half of cross stitch	
────	Outer border Very Fine #4 Braid 001C, couched	
────	Inner border 232/452 backstitch, 1 strand	

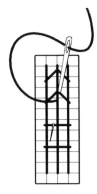

Fig 1 Couching

To work the dragonfly wings:

6 Refer to the dragonfly chart and wings key for the specific threads and stitches for each part. Work the stitches in the order listed in the key. When couching bring the thread to be couched up at the right and hold in place with your left thumb while working. Keeping the distance between stitches consistent, stitch in place with small couching stitches (see Couching, page 37). Repeat until all couched thread is secured. Plunge the ends to the back and secure.

7 Once all the stitching is complete, insert the design into a suitable box following the manufacturer's instructions. Alternatively it could be mounted in a picture frame.

BACKGROUND CHART

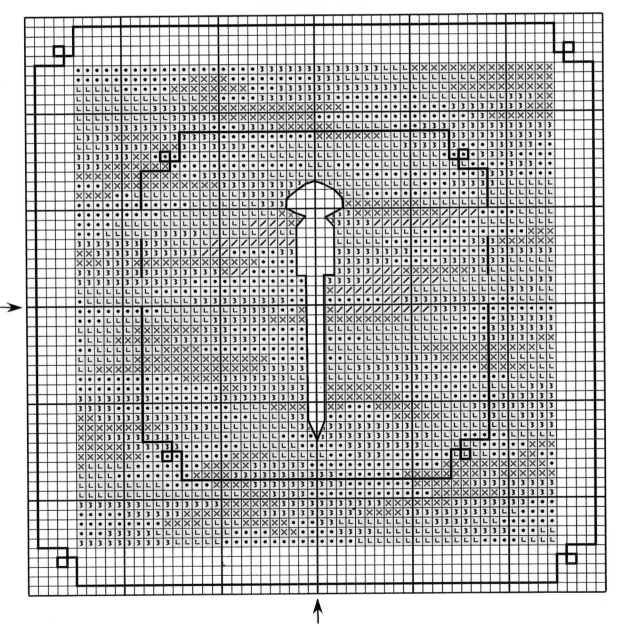

BUTTERCUP BOUQUET

Designed by Merrilyn Heazlewood, Australia

THIS CHARMING SACHET ILLUSTRATES THE SOFT EFFECTS OF METALLIC RIBBONS USED IN TRADITIONAL RIBBON EMBROIDERY. EASE OF HANDLING, SOFTNESS AND DURABILITY ARE CHARACTERISTICS OF THE METALLIC THREADS THAT ENABLE THE EMBROIDERER TO CONTROL EACH STITCH WITH CONFIDENCE. THE RIBBONS LAY WHERE POSITIONED WITHOUT BUCKLING OR RESISTING. METALLIC RIBBONS HAVE AN INHERENT FLEXIBILITY; FOR FRENCH KNOTS THEY PROVIDE A STABLE KNOT THAT WILL NOT FLATTEN OVER TIME. METALLIC RIBBONS ALSO MAINTAIN THEIR LOFT AND COLOUR EVEN AFTER MANY MACHINE-, HAND- OR DRY-CLEANINGS.

Stitching Notes

Design Size: 7 x 10cm (2¾ x 4in) approximately
Finished Size of Sachet: 12.75 x 17cm (5 x 7in)

YOU WILL NEED

- Two pieces 23.5 x 15cm (9¼ x 6in) of ivory Damask Rose fabric
- Kreinik ¹⁄₁₆" Ribbon: 9100 Sunlight, 026 Amethyst, 326 Hibiscus, 102C Vatican Gold
- Kreinik ⅛" Ribbon: 012 Purple, 091 Star Yellow
- Kreinik Very Fine (#4) Braid 009 Emerald
- Anchor/DMC stranded cotton (floss) 295/726 (yellow)
- Anchor/DMC pearl cotton No.8 214/368 (green)
- Ivory ½in satin ribbon for tie, 20cm (8in)

1   Take one of the pieces of fabric and fold it in half lengthways to find the centre. Measure 10cm (4in) down from the top edge for the placement of the top centre gold sprinkle (French knot). The design is stitched from here, on the right side of the fabric.

Copy the design on to the fabric using the stitch diagram on page 70 – see step 1, page 77. Begin working the design from the stitch diagram.

2   Stitch the buttercups in lazy daisy stitches (Fig 1) in Sunlight ¹⁄₁₆" Ribbon, filled in with three or four straight stitches using a full strand of yellow stranded cotton (floss) 295/726. Then stitch the buttercup buds in Star Yellow ⅛" Ribbon in ribbon stitch (Fig 2).

Fig 1 Lazy daisy stitch: Come up at 1 and down at 2, holding the thread in a loop. Take a small stitch at 3–4 to secure the stitch in the desired location

Fig 2 Ribbon stitch: Come up at 1 and pierce the ribbon at 2. Pull the needle to the back gently and allow the edges of the ribbon to curl at the tip

Fig 3 Merrilyn's bow: Form the bow with two horizontal lazy daisy stitches, connected with one cross stitch above two straight stitches (which have a slight twist)

3   Stitch the irises by working the top of the flower in a lazy daisy stitch in Hibiscus ⅟₁₆" Ribbon. Then work a curved stitch running underneath the base of the lazy daisy stitch in the same colour ribbon.

4   Stitch the violets by working each petal in ribbon stitch in Amethyst ⅟₁₆" Ribbon. Work single French knots in yellow stranded cotton (floss) for the centres.

5   Work the flower stems in straight stitches with the green No.8 pearl cotton 214/368. Then work the leaves in straight stitches with Emerald Very Fine (#4) Braid.

6   Stitch the gold 'sprinkles' with single French knots in ⅟₁₆" Ribbon Vatican Gold. Finally, stitch a Merrilyn's Bow (see Fig 3) in Purple ⅛" Ribbon.

To make up the sachet:

7   Take the unembroidered piece of fabric and put it right sides together with the embroidered piece. Sew a 1.25cm (½in) seam down the sides and across the bottom of the pieces. Still with wrong sides outwards, turn under a 6mm (¼in) edge at the top of the bag and press to the wrong side. Next, turn down a 4cm (1½in) of the fabric and stitch close to the bottom of this fold. Measure 2cm

(¾in) up from the edge of this fold and stitch another row to make a casing. On the bottom edge of the bag, fold the fabric so that the side seams and bottom seam match, forming a triangle. In the seam allowance sew across the bottom edge of the triangle on both bottom corners – this will form a flat bottom on the bag. Turn the bag right side out. Remove a few stitches at one of the casing seams to make an opening to insert the ribbon tie. Insert the length of ivory satin ribbon, leaving a tail to tie into a bow. Your sachet is now complete.

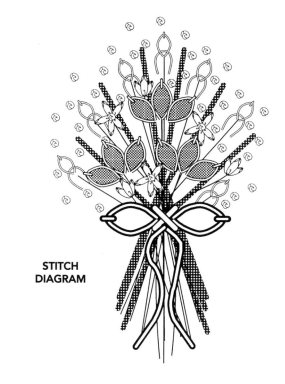

STITCH DIAGRAM

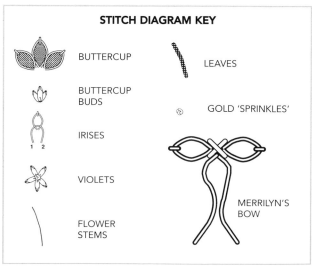

STITCH DIAGRAM KEY

	BUTTERCUP	LEAVES
	BUTTERCUP BUDS	
	IRISES	GOLD 'SPRINKLES'
	VIOLETS	
	FLOWER STEMS	MERRILYN'S BOW

ROMANCE SAMPLER

Designed by Emie Bishop, USA

THE ROMANCE SAMPLER IS A CAREFULLY ORCHESTRATED SERIES OF STITCHES DESIGNED TO DEVELOP UNDERSTANDING AND MASTERY OF THE VARIOUS EFFECTS ACHIEVED BY USING KREINIK METALLIC THREADS. THE DESIGN SHOWS THAT METALLIC THREADS CAN ADD A DELICATE FEEL AND A REFINED, SOPHISTICATED ELEGANCE TO CLASSIC EMBROIDERY.

THE SAMPLER FEATURES A WEALTH OF INTERESTING STITCHES. BACKSTITCHES AND QUEEN STITCHES WORKED IN BLENDING FILAMENT PRODUCE AN UNPARALLELED DELICACY UNACHIEVABLE WITH OTHER THREADS, WHILE OLD-FASHIONED HEMSTITCH BRACKETS CLASSIC FIFTEENTH CENTURY ASSISI-STYLE EMBROIDERY. THE BORDER CREATES A FRAME OF PURE SILVER CLARITY ADDING TO THE DESIGN'S OVERALL DELICACY AND MAGIC. USING METALLIC THREADS IN CLASSIC SAMPLER EMBROIDERY IS REMINISCENT OF ANTIQUE SAMPLERS WHEN REAL METAL THREADS WERE USED. (SEE PICTURE DETAILS ON PAGES 26 AND 42.)

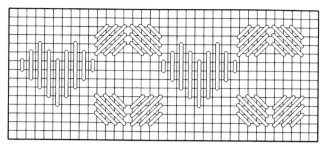

Fig 1 Band 2 – satin stitch hearts and cushion on linen blocks

Stitching Notes

Stitch Count: 80 stitches wide x 118 high

Design Size: 14.5 x 21.5cm (5¾ x 8½in) on 28 count

Each square on the chart represents two fabric threads, while the lines on the stitch diagram (Fig 1, right) represent single fabric threads.

Refer to Chapter 3 for working the stitches.

YOU WILL NEED

- 35.5 x 43cm (14 x 17in) antique white 28 count linen
- Kreinik Silk Mori® 8000 White
- Kreinik Silk Mori® 1032 Lightest Pink
- Kreinik Blending Filament 092 Star Pink
- Kreinik Very Fine (#4) Braid 192 Pale Pink
- Kreinik Fine (#8) Braid 9200 Blossom
- Kreinik ⅛" Ribbon 032 Pearl
- Kreinik #1 Japan Thread 001J Silver
- Kreinik Cable 001P Silver
- Anchor/DMC stranded cotton (floss): 23/818, 24/776, 36/3326, 38/335, 261/3053, 262/3052, 681/3051,
- Anchor/DMC No.8 pearl cotton, 2/White
- Anchor/DMC No.12 pearl cotton, 2/White

To work band 1:

1   Prepare your fabric and begin working from the top of the chart. Complete all the cross stitches using two strands of stranded cotton (floss) worked over two threads, following the symbols on the chart and key.

Fill in the centre section of the heart with an alternating cross stitch using two strands of Blending Filament 092 to create a dimensional texture and allow a subtle shimmer to spread over the surface. (This effect can be achieved anywhere on any design with any colour.)

To work band 2:

2   Satin stitch the hearts with two strands of pink Silk Mori® 1032.

Use two strands of white Silk Mori® 8000 for the cushion on linen stitches between the hearts (shown in the stitch diagram in Fig 1).

To work band 3:

3   Use a single strand of Blending Filament 092 for the backstitch border and the same thread and single strand for the Queen stitch centres of the band.

To work band 4:

4   Stitch the four-sided stitch over Pearl ⅛" Ribbon 032. Start by bringing the ribbon from the back, across the row, and reinsert the end on the other side of the row. Then, using Very Fine (#4) Braid 192 work four-sided stitches across the top of the ribbon.

To work band 5:

5   Work the band of swirling satin stitches in Fine (#8) Braid 9200 Blossom (see diagram and picture, page 42).

To work band 6:

6   Completely remove one of the threads (shown as 6A on the chart). Cut the second thread of 6A in the centre of the row. Weave it back into the place formerly occupied by the thread that was removed. Remove thread 6B in the same way. Now, using white No.12 pearl cotton, complete an old-fashioned hemstitch along 6A and 6B.

Use two strands of stranded cotton (floss) 23/818 for the cross stitches in the Assisi background. Backstitch the Assisi pattern inside the row using a single strand of Blending Filament 092.

Repeat the hemstitching as described above, this time below the Assisi pattern, as shown on the chart.

To work band 7:

7   Create the crisp, delicate detail of the short, central line of four-sided stitches with Silver Japan #1.

Using white No.8 pearl cotton, complete the satin

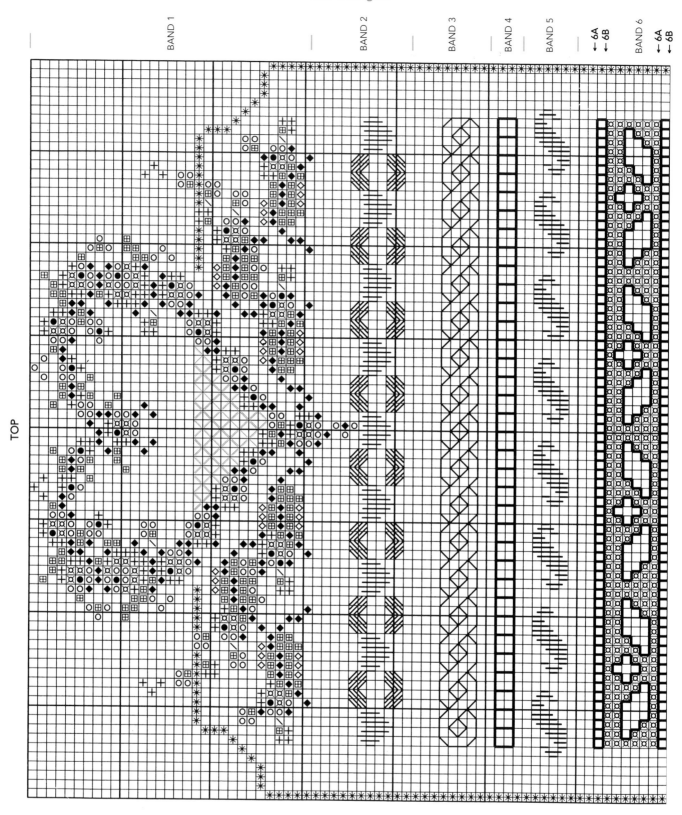

stitch tulips and the leaf stitches. Then use white No.12 pearl cotton for the bullion stitch centres of the tulips.

Use Silver Japan Thread #1 for the four-sided stitches (do not pull these). (See picture, page 26.)

Use white No.8 pearl cotton for the Kloster blocks.

Be careful to cut the correct threads along the side bars of Kloster blocks. Cut the four fabric threads next to the corner dove's eye, leave four fabric threads, cut four more (as indicated by the line break on the chart), leave four more and cut the last four next to the corner dove's

BAND 7

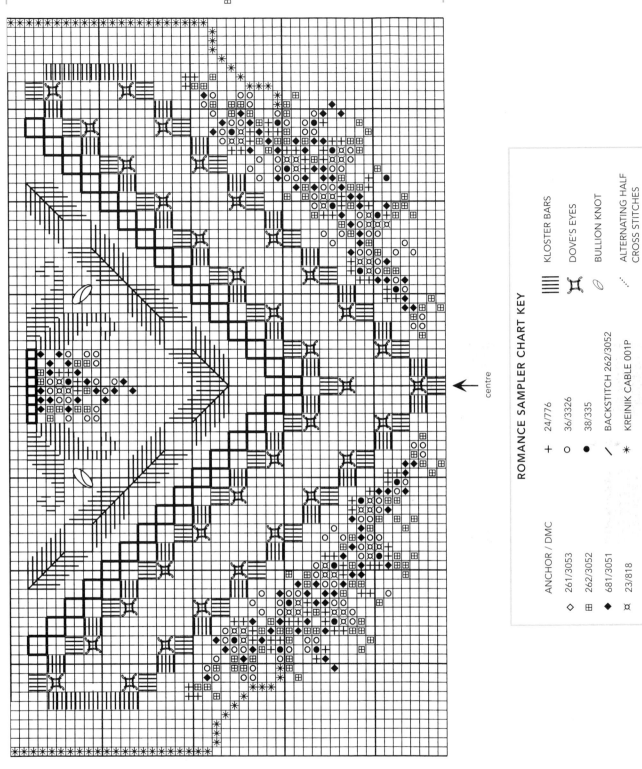

centre

ROMANCE SAMPLER CHART KEY

ANCHOR / DMC		
◇	261/3053	
⊞	262/3052	
◆	681/3051	
¤	23/818	
+	24/776	
○	36/3326	
●	38/335	
/	BACKSTITCH 262/3052	
*	KREINIK CABLE 001P	

⫴⫴⫴	KLOSTER BARS	
⋈	DOVE'S EYES	
∅	BULLION KNOT	
⋯	ALTERNATING HALF CROSS STITCHES	

eye. Continue cutting around the Kloster blocks, using the corner dove's eye as your guide. (Cut against the end of the Kloster stitches, not the sides.) Using white No.12 pearl cotton, complete the Hardanger pattern of wrapped bars and corner dove's eyes.

Finally, use two strands of stranded cotton (floss) for the cross stitches, following the colours given in the key.

8 Finish by cross stitching the border with Cable 001P, then prepare your sampler for mounting and framing.

POPPIES, SNAILS AND PEACOCKS' TAILS

Designed by Susie Johns, UK

METALLIC THREADS DRAW THE EYE INTO THE CENTRE OF THIS CONTEMPORARY EMBROIDERY. THERE ARE THREE POPPIES, SNAILS AND TAILS AND EACH FEATURES A CIRCULAR SHAPE. THESE MOTIFS HAVE NOT BEEN CHOSEN MERELY FOR THEIR COMPLEMENTARY SHAPES HOWEVER; PEACOCK FEATHERS HAVE A WONDERFUL IRIDESCENCE. COMBINE THIS WITH THE GLOSS OF A POPPY'S PETALS AND THE SHINE ON A SNAIL'S SHELL – NOT TO MENTION THE SILVER TRAIL IT LEAVES IN ITS WAKE – AND YOU HAVE A SUBJECT THAT CRIES OUT FOR THE SHIMMER OF METALLIC THREADS. THOUGH THE SHAPES ARE HEAVILY EMBROIDERED, THIS DESIGN IS SATISFYINGLY QUICK AND EASY TO STITCH AND CAN EVEN BE ATTEMPTED BY A BEGINNER TO SURFACE EMBROIDERY. STRETCH YOUR FABRIC IN AN EMBROIDERY HOOP OR FRAME TO AVOID PUCKERING AND DISTORTION, AND DON'T BE AFRAID TO MIX THREAD COLOURS TO PRODUCE A SHADED EFFECT, PARTICULARLY ON THE PETALS.

Stitching Notes

Stitch Count: 160 stitches wide x 224 high
Design Size: 12.5 x 17.5cm (5 x 7in)
Code numbers on Fig 1 refer to Anchor stranded cotton (floss), while type and code are given for Kreinik threads.

YOU WILL NEED

- 28 x 33cm (11 x 13in) piece blue 32 count linen
- Kreinik Blending Filament: 001 Silver, 043 Confetti Green
- Kreinik Cord 051C Sapphire
- Kreinik Very Fine (#4) Braid 002C Gold
- Kreinik Fine (#8) Braid 005HL Black Hi-Lustre
- Kreinik Ombre 3200 Solid Pearl
- Anchor/DMC stranded cotton (floss): 13/817, 20/3777, 27/894, 28/956, 29/309, 46/666, 238/703, 253/472, 293/727, 307/783, 309/708, 335/606, 433/996, 940/797, 779/931, 9046/321
- Handmade edging cord (optional)

1 Begin by tracing Fig 1 (the design outline) on page 78 on to paper, using a sharp pencil and tracing paper. Do not trace the thread and stitch instructions. On the reverse of the paper, go over the lines with a transfer pen (red or orange will show up quite well on dark blue fabric). Place the tracing in the centre of your fabric, right side up. Ensure that the border lines correspond with the warp and weft threads of the fabric, so the design is straight. Press with a hot iron to transfer the design on to the fabric, and then mount the fabric in an embroidery hoop or frame.

2 The design is filled in using the design outline in Fig 1 as a guide to threads and colours. Using two strands of stranded cotton (floss), start by stitching a backstitch line around the border of the design using two strands of 238/703, following the weave of the fabric to ensure the lines are straight.

335 & 9046

20
20
20

46
433 940

FILLED WITH 335
THEN OVERLAID
WITH FINE BRAID
005HL

335
335
335
335
335 & 9046
335
&
29
335
&
29

20

20
9046 & 20

20

20

CENTRE: 20, 293
NARROW RING:
253

SNAIL TRAIL:
OMBRE 3200
COUCHED
WITH KBF 001

13

13
&
20

9046
433
940

NARROW RING:
293

20 & 29

20

CENTRE: 9046,
293
NARROW RING:
238, 253

238

FEATHER FRONDS:
940, 051C, KBF 043

293

293
&
307

293
&
307

27

779

NARROW RING:
253 & 238

27 & 29

335 & 27

29

27
&
29

29   27

27 & 28

27

433
940
9046

NARROW RING:
293

238

28 & 29

27

307 & 309

307

293 & 307

307 & 309

238

OUTLINE SHELLS IN BACKSTITCH
VERY FINE BRAID 002C

Fig 1 Design outline

3 Now fill in the various shapes on the design. Fill in small shapes with satin stitch and the larger shapes, such as the flower petals, with long and short satin stitch, with stitch lines radiating out from the centre. (See Chapter 3 for working the stitches.) Following the threads and colours listed on Fig 1, overlay flower centres with Black Hi-Lustre Fine (#8) Braid, and highlight some of the petals with Blending Filament (abbreviated to KBF on the diagram) to add an extra sparkle.

Where two thread code numbers occur together on the diagram, such as in the flower petals, blend them together using the two different coloured strands in your needle at the same time.

4 Outline the snail shells in backstitch with Very Fine (#4) Braid 002C Gold. Stitch the feather fronds in stem stitch, combining Sapphire Cord 051C with stranded cotton (floss) as you stitch, or adding it later. Lastly, add the snail trail, couching a length of Pearl Ombre with Silver Blending Filament to give a smooth line. You could copy the trail in the photograph or work your own freehand.

5 Your embroidered design is now finished. As shown, you could edge it with a blue and red twisted cord made from metallic braids and silks and then stitch it on to a red padded frame. Alternatively, place the design within a frame and mount of your choice.

SLEEPING MERMAID AND RAINBOW FISHES

Designed by Susie Johns, UK

METALLIC THREADS ARE USED TO HIGHLIGHT
AND ENHANCE HEAVILY WORKED AREAS OF SATIN
STITCH IN THIS SURFACE EMBROIDERY DESIGN.
FIRST, THE WHOLE DESIGN IS FILLED IN WITH
STRANDED COTTON (FLOSS), WITH SHADING AND
BLENDING ACHIEVED BY USING TWO DIFFERENT
COLOURED THREADS IN THE NEEDLE.
THEN SPARKLING METALLIC THREADS, IN JEWEL TONES
AND RAINBOW SHADES, ARE USED TO OUTLINE
CERTAIN AREAS. STARBURST FINE BRAID, FOR EXAMPLE,
OUTLINES EACH SCALE ON THE MERMAID'S TAIL AND
PRODUCES AN IRIDESCENT EFFECT, WHILE
STRANDS OF STAR PINK FINE BRAID AND ORANGE
BLENDING FILAMENT ARE WOVEN THROUGH HER
HAIR TO MAKE IT GLEAM.

Stitching Notes

Stitch Count: *224 stitches wide x 160 high*
Design Size: *18 x 12.5cm (7 x 5in)*
*Code numbers on Fig 1 refer to Anchor stranded cotton
(floss), while the Kreinik threads are noted by their type
and code.*
Refer to Chapter 3 for working the stitches.

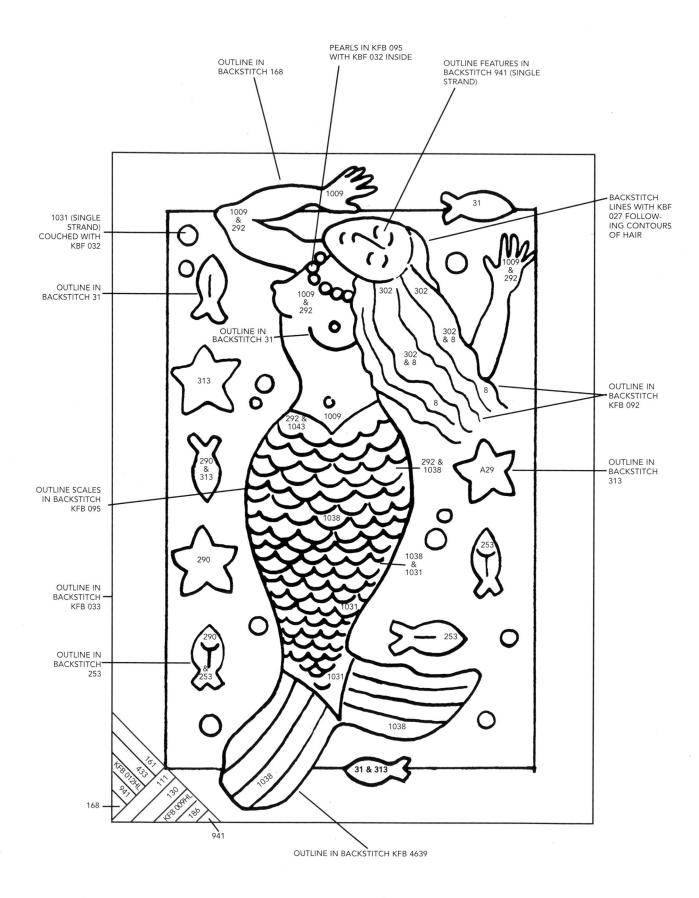

PEARLS IN KFB 095
WITH KBF 032 INSIDE

OUTLINE IN
BACKSTITCH 168

OUTLINE FEATURES IN
BACKSTITCH 941 (SINGLE
STRAND)

BACKSTITCH
LINES WITH KBF
027 FOLLOW-
ING CONTOURS
OF HAIR

1031 (SINGLE
STRAND)
COUCHED WITH
KBF 032

OUTLINE IN
BACKSTITCH 31

OUTLINE IN
BACKSTITCH 31

OUTLINE IN
BACKSTITCH
KFB 092

OUTLINE SCALES
IN BACKSTITCH
KFB 095

OUTLINE IN
BACKSTITCH
313

OUTLINE IN
BACKSTITCH
KFB 033

OUTLINE IN
BACKSTITCH
253

OUTLINE IN BACKSTITCH KFB 4639

Fig 1 Design outline

YOU WILL NEED

- 33 x 28cm (13 x 11in) piece of blue 32 count linen
- Kreinik Blending Filament: 027 Orange, 032 Pearl
- Kreinik Fine (#8) Braid: 033 Royal Blue, 092 Star Pink, 095 Starburst, 4639 Light Aqua, 012HL Purple Hi-Lustre, 009HL Emerald Hi-Lustre
- Anchor/DMC stranded cotton (floss): 8/353, 31/957, 111/208, 130/799, 161/516, 168/597, 186/959 253/472, 290/973, 292/3078, 302/743, 313/3827, 433/996, 941/792, 1009/3770, 1031/775, 1038/519, 1043/369
- Kreinik Silver Torsade (optional)

1 Begin by tracing Fig 1 (the design outline) on page 82 on to paper, using a sharp pencil and tracing paper (see step 1, page 76).

2 The design is filled in using Fig 1 as a guide to threads and colours, with two strands of stranded cotton (floss) used. Start by backstitching both border lines using Fine (#8) Braid 033, following the weave of the fabric to ensure the lines are straight.

Work the border, stitching the stripes in satin stitch, following the colours and pattern given in Fig 1 (bottom left corner).

3 Fill in the fish and starfish in satin stitch, using stranded cotton (floss) colours according to Fig 1. Where two code numbers occur together on the diagram, blend them together using the two different coloured strands in your needle at the same time.

Fill in the mermaid's scales in satin stitch, starting at the top with one strand of 292/3078 and one of 1043/369 in your needle. After two rows, change the thread to one strand of 292/3078 and one of 1038/519. Then change to two strands of 1038/519, and so on, to produce a graduated colour.

Stitch the mermaid's fins, hair, body, and face in long and short stitch, again blending colours in your needle where indicated on Fig 1.

4 To add highlights, outline using backstitch with Fine Braid as follows: scales 095; fins 4639; hair 092. Stitch her pearls by backstitching the circles in Fine Braid 095, filling in with satin stitches in Blending Filament 032. For the bubbles, use a single strand of 1031/775 couched with 032 Blending Filament (abbreviated on the diagram to KBF); this produces a smoother, rounder contour than if you worked it in backstitch.

5 Your embroidered design is now finished. As shown in the photograph, you could edge it with a silver Torsade and mount it on a padded board, or place the design within a frame and mount of your choice.

Simply using metallic thread can alter the way a design detail is seen, as in the mermaid's hair. Try adding a Blending Filament, Cord, Braid or Ribbon and watch your creativity personalise any design

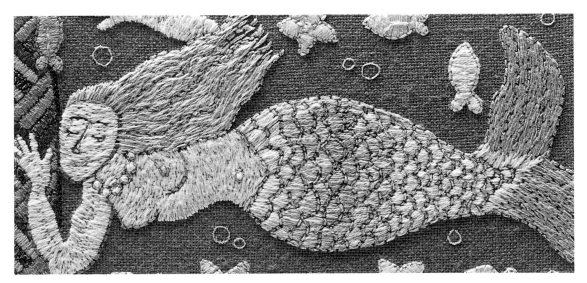

CLASSIC GOLDEN BALANTINE

Original design by Pat Hollister, New Zealand, adapted by Ann Caswell

A 'BALANTINE' OR SMALL BAG THAT HUNG FROM A CORD OR CHAIN WAS POPULAR IN THE EARLY NINETEENTH CENTURY. THEY WERE MADE IN MATERIALS THAT RANGED FROM VELVET OR SILK STRETCHED OVER EMBOSSED CARDBOARD, TO LACE ALTERNATING STRANDS OF REAL GOLD AND SILVER THREADS. METAL THREAD WORK IS STILL A VIABLE TECHNIQUE BUT TRUE METALS ARE EXPENSIVE AND TIME CONSUMING TO MANUFACTURE AND THEY REQUIRE SKILFUL APPLICATION. MATERIALS FOR GOLD WORK TODAY INCLUDE ALL KINDS OF SHINING SYNTHETIC EMBROIDERY THREADS THAT ARE MORE MALLEABLE, VERSATILE AND EASY TO USE. SOME MAY EVEN BE WASHED AND IRONED.

THIS PROJECT ILLUSTRATES HOW EASY IT IS TO SIMULATE THE LOOK OF REAL METAL THREAD EMBROIDERY USING SYNTHETIC METALLIC THREADS. TWO METHODS OF COUCHING ARE COMBINED WITH ROWS OF SIMPLE STITCHES TO CREATE AN ELEGANT EVENING HANDBAG (IT IS ALSO SUITABLE FOR A DIGNIFIED CUMMERBUND). THE SPRINKLING OF REAL METAL PAILLETTES ON THE BACK ILLUSTRATES HOW EASY IT IS TO ADD A UNIQUE DETAIL INTO YOUR EMBROIDERY WITH A SIMPLE FRENCH KNOT.

Stitching Notes

Design Size: *72 stitches wide x 88 long*

Finished Size: *approximately 10 x 12.5cm (4 x 5in) on 18 count canvas*

Each line on the diagram represents one canvas thread.

Refer to Chapter 3 for working the stitches.

YOU WILL NEED

- Two pieces of 18 x 20cm (7 x 8in) brown 18 count Mono Deluxe canvas
- Kreinik Cord 002C Gold
- Kreinik Very Fine (#4) Braid 102C Vatican Gold
- Kreinik Tapestry (#12) Braid: 001C Silver; 205C Antique Gold
- Kreinik ⅟₁₆" Ribbon: 001C Silver 10m (10¾yd), 102C Vatican Gold 20m (22yd)
- Kreinik ⅛" Ribbon 102C Vatican Gold 5m (5½yd)
- Kreinik Silk Mori® 8050 Black 38m (41yd) (this is sufficient for the tassels too)
- Kreinik Gold and Silver Paillettes (Spangles) #14, 3mm
- Kreinik 4mm Torsade, Antique Gold/Silver/Gold (for a shoulder strap)
- Lightweight lining fabric (e.g. UltraSuede)

To work the front of the bag:

1   Prepare one of your pieces of 18 count canvas for work, mounting it on to stretcher bars and making it drum tight.

2   Follow the stitch diagram on page 87 for the front of the bag: the area shown is half the width of the bag (the centre is indicated by the arrow). Repeat the entire pattern three times for the length of the bag.

Rows 1–2: Work tent stitch in Tapestry (#12) Braid 205C.

Rows 3–5: Couch 1⁄16" Ribbon 102C with a single strand of Cord 002C.

Row 6: Stitch the large cross of the rice stitch (indicated by the black stitches) with 1⁄16" Ribbon 001C and cross the corners (indicated by the smaller white stitches) with 1⁄16" Ribbon 102C.

Rows 7–8: Work tent stitch in Tapestry (#12) Braid 001C.

Row 9: Work alternating mosaic stitches in 1⁄16" Ribbon 102C.

Rows 10–11: Work tent stitch in Tapestry (#12) Braid 001C.

Row 12: Work cross stitch in 1⁄16" Ribbon 102C.

Rows 13–16: Work tent stitch in three strands of Silk Mori® 8050.

Row 17: Couch 1⁄8" Ribbon 102C with Very Fine (#4) Braid 102C.

Rows 18–21: Work tent stitch in three strands of Silk Mori® 8050.

Row 22: Work cross stitch in 1⁄16" Ribbon 102C.

Repeat these twenty-two rows three more times to complete the front of the bag.

To work the back of the bag:

3   Prepare your second piece of canvas for work, as described in Step 1. Then follow the stitch diagram for the back of the bag. The back repeats the couching rows as shown on the front (Rows 3–5 and 17). Stitch all other rows in tent stitch (basketweave) in black Silk Mori®.

Attach gold and silver paillettes in alternating rows with French knots using two strands of black Silk Mori® (shown by circles on the stitch diagram).

Finishing the bag:

4   Whipstitch the front of the bag to the back piece, matching the couching rows – the canvas size given in the supplies list is sufficient for a 4cm (1½in) seam allowance. Determine the desired length of the shoulder strap made from Kreinik Torsade and attach the ends inside the top sides of the bag.

5   Make two 18cm (7in) tassels of black Silk Mori®. Cut a 19cm (7½in) piece of sturdy cardboard, then cut

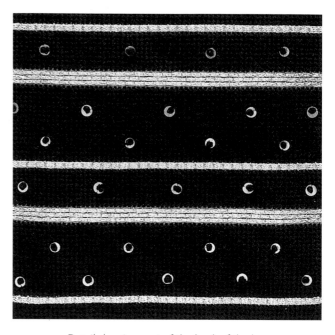

Detail showing part of the back of the bag with rows of couching and basketweave stitch. This part of the bag could be worked in other combinations of stitches (see some of the many choices available on pages 36–43)

a 10cm (4in) length of the Silk Mori® to act as a hanger and a 15cm (6in) length of 1⁄8" Ribbon as a wrapping. Wrap the black Silk Mori® many times round the cardboard to reach the desired thickness. Slip the 10cm (4in) length of Silk Mori® under the loops at the top of the cardboard and tie tightly, gathering the loops. Cut the loops at the other end. Holding the tassel securely about 2.5cm (1in) below the top, wrap the piece of Ribbon several times around the threads to create the neck of the tassel. Tuck the ends of the Ribbon inside the tassel using a needle and neatly trim the ends of the tassel. Once both tassels are made, attach them at the outside top sides of the bag.

6   Construct a lining bag, made of a lightweight fabric of your choice, and carefully insert it into the embroidered bag, neatly whipstitching it to the top edges of the bag. To finish, make a fine twisted cord of black Silk Mori® and stitch it around both sides, the bottom and both top edges to provide an elegant and sophisticated finish.

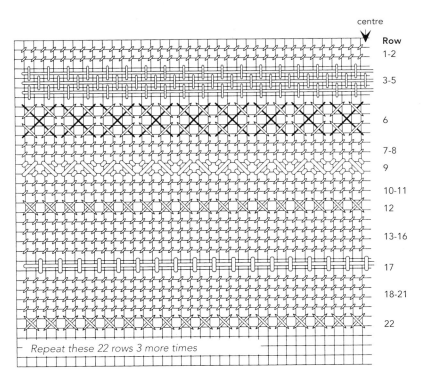

centre

	Row
	1-2
	3-5
	6
	7-8
	9
	10-11
	12
	13-16
	17
	18-21
	22

Repeat these 22 rows 3 more times

Stitch Diagram – front of bag

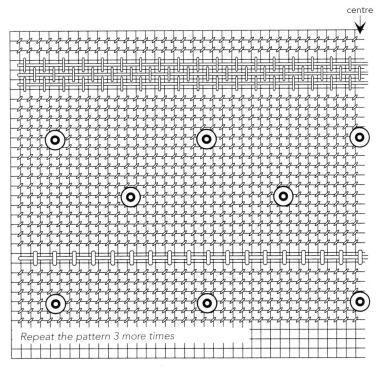

centre

Repeat the pattern 3 more times

Stitch Diagram – back of bag

FOUR SEASONS PATCHWORK GIRLS

Designed by Mary Polityka Bush, USA

FOUR SEASONS IS A WONDERFUL COLLECTION
OF SPIRITED DESIGNS THAT WILL ENTICE YOU TO
DEVELOP YOUR STITCHING SKILLS AND APPRECIATION
FOR METALLIC THREADS. WHETHER YOU WANT TO
RECREATE NATURE'S LIGHT SOURCE OR SIMPLY ADD
PLAYFUL TEXTURE AND DIMENSION, METALLIC
THREADS ENABLE THE STITCHER TO USE DIFFERENT
STITCH TECHNIQUES TO CREATE VARIOUS TEXTURES,
HIGHLIGHTS, DEPTH, AND ABOVE ALL – WONDERMENT.
SILVER AND SAPPHIRE FACETS™ ARE USED TO CREATE
THE FRAME IN EACH DESIGN TO ENCAPSULATE THE
MOMENTS OF THE FOUR SEASONS THAT SET
THE CYCLE OF OUR LIVES.

Stitching Notes

Stitch Count (for each design): *96 stitches x 127*
Design Size (for each design): *10 x 13.5cm (4 x 5¼in)*
Refer to Chapter 3 for working the stitches.
*Keep the wrong side of the embroidery as neat as
possible. Do not travel from one area to another behind
unworked areas of canvas. Trim all thread tails closely.
A tiny dab of washable glue may help tame unruly
thread tails.*
*The set of four canvas embroideries requires only one
reel or one skein of each of the colours/threads listed
even if the same colour/thread is used in more than one
embroidery. Exceptions are noted in parentheses.*

SPRING PATCHWORK GIRL

Metallics not only create a realistic rainfall but also the smooth and slippery raincoat (slicker) that protects our little child. The freshness of a spring shower is captured in the raindrops, the umbrella and the Hi-Lustre boots. This is a fun piece.

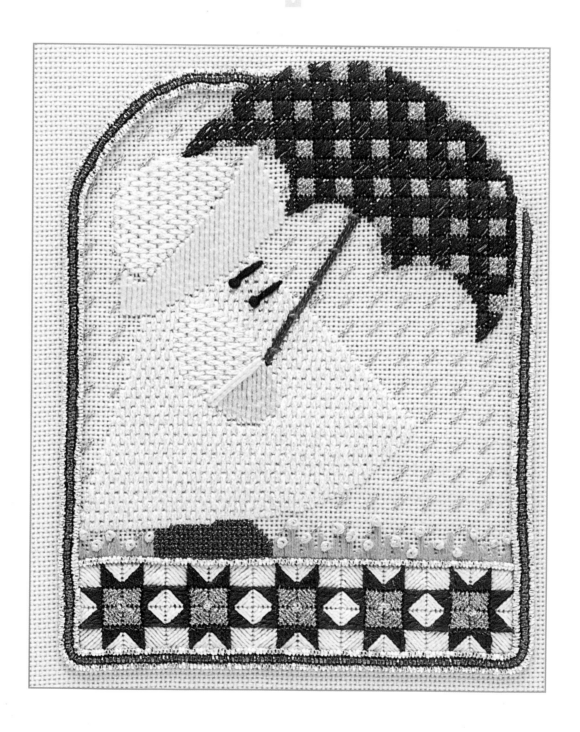

YOU WILL NEED

- 25.5 x 28cm (10 x 11in) piece of pale blue 24 count Congress Cloth (Zweigart 9406/594)
- Kreinik Blending Filament 012HL Purple Hi-Lustre
- Kreinik Very Fine (#4) Braid 014 Sky Blue
- Kreinik Fine (#8) Braid 001HL Silver Hi-Lustre; 003 Red, 015 Chartreuse
- Kreinik Tapestry (#12) Braid 091 Star Yellow (2 reels)
- Kreinik Cord 001C Silver, 051C Sapphire
- Kreinik Facets™ Silver (2 skeins), Sapphire
- Anchor/DMC stranded cotton (floss): 85/3609, 102/550, 256/704, 403/310,
- Anchor/DMC No.8 pearl cotton: 2/White, 401/413
- Anchor/DMC No.5 pearl cotton: 102/550, 295/726, 1012/754

Preparing the canvas:

1   Lay the canvas over the stitching outline diagram (see pages 99–100: Fig 1 Spring, Fig 2 Summer, Fig 3 Autumn or Fig 4 Winter) and trace it carefully using a hard pencil. If it is difficult to see the line drawing in the book through the canvas, photocopy it and tape it to a window or lay it on a light box. Then tape or lay the canvas over the photocopy and trace. Once the canvas has been marked with the design, mount it on stretcher bars, pulling it drum tight.

To work the umbrella:

2   Prepare your canvas as described above (using Fig 1 on page 99), and begin by using Fine (#8) Braid 015 to fill the umbrella with Scotch stitches over four canvas threads, leaving four canvas threads unworked on each side of each stitch unit. Compensate the stitches as necessary along the curves. Refer to Chapter 3 for how to work the stitches.

Use one strand of Blending Filament 012HL together with three strands of 102/550 stranded cotton (floss) to fill the remaining area of the umbrella with Scotch stitches.

Use No.8 pearl cotton 401/413 to work three long straight stitches for the handle, couching all three as one with short, perpendicular straight stitches every 0.5cm (¼in).

To work the hat, coat, hand and boot:

3   Use Tapestry (#12) Braid 091 to fill the hat crown, coat and sleeve areas with brick stitch over four canvas threads. To define the sleeve on a garment, stitch its pattern in the direction opposite that of the coat or dress (see photograph, left). Stitch the hat in the same direction as the sleeve.

Use No.5 pearl cotton 295/726 to fill the hat brim area with vertical straight stitches and to work two straight stitches for the sleeve cuff.

Use No.5 pearl cotton 1012/754 to fill the hand area with vertical straight stitches.

Use four strands of stranded cotton (floss) 403/310 to work a straight stitch with a French knot at the end for each coat closure, wrapping the needle twice for each knot.

Use Fine (#8) Braid 003 to fill the boot area with basketweave stitch.

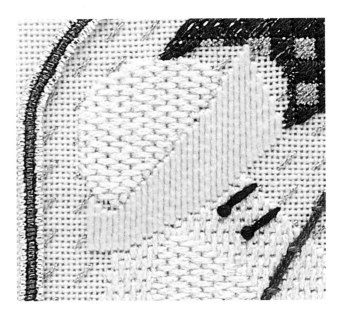

To work the rain, grass and flowers:

4   Use Very Fine (#4) Braid 014 to fill the sky with diagonal darning. Turn around at the outer edges of the area by making tiny running stitches along the path that will be covered with the Facets™ outline.

Use four strands of stranded cotton (floss) 256/704 to fill the grass area with random-length straight stitches.

Use four strands of stranded cotton (floss) 85/3609 to randomly place French knot flowers in the grass, wrapping the needle twice for each knot.

To work the star panel:

5　Start by leaving one canvas thread bare between the grass and the star panel (a length of Silver Facets™ will be couched along here later). With reference to the star panel stitch diagram (right), and using Fine (#8) Braid 015, work four Scotch stitches for the centre of each star. Slant the star border stitches in the directions indicated on the stitch diagram.

　　　Use No.5 pearl cotton 102/550 to work the points of the stars in satin stitches.

　　　Use No.8 pearl cotton 2/white to fill the area around the stars with Scotch and half-Scotch stitches.

　　　Use Fine (#8) Braid 001HL to centre each star with a French knot.

6　Cut a piece of Silver Facets™ 5cm (2in) longer than the mesh between the grass and the star panel. Wrapping the Facets™ tightly with clear tape before cutting helps prevent raveling. Cut through the centre of the piece of tape; do not remove it afterward. Use a No.18 needle to gently enlarge a hole at each end of the bare canvas mesh. Lay the Facets™ along the mesh, carefully plunging the tape-wrapped ends to the wrong side of the embroidery. If it is difficult to push the Facets™ through the canvas, thread it into the eye of the needle and pull it through. On the wrong side of the embroidery, fold the ends of the Facets™ along its travelling path on the right side. Use Cord 001C (locked in the eye of the needle) to couch the Facets™ with short, perpendicular stitches every 3mm (⅛in), securing the ends of the Facets™ with the couching stitches. Give each couching stitch a very gentle tug to pop it down between the twists of the Facets™.

To work the design outline:

7　Beginning with the innermost row, follow the same procedure to work the outline around the whole design. Couch three rows of Facets™ – first Silver, then Sapphire and then Silver again, noting that the Facets™ stops on each side of the umbrella, allowing it to break out of the outline (see photograph on page 90). Place couching stitches closer together along curves and at corners. The embroidery can now be framed.

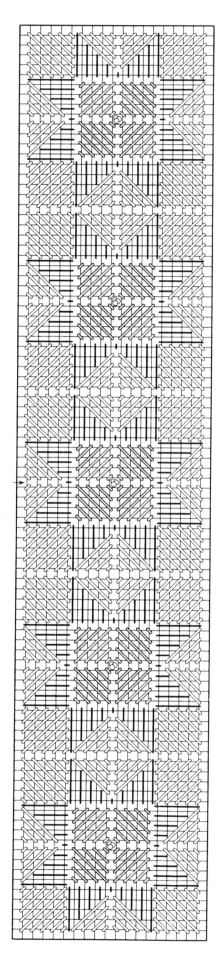

Star panel stitch diagram
(Each line on the diagram represents one canvas thread)

92

SUMMER PATCHWORK GIRL

The sunflower radiates from petals that spread out under the warmth of the summer sun.
Using Hi-Lustre creates accents in the colourful dress to reinforce the contrast that different threads give to
embroidery. A soft ribbon falls across the dress to give an elegant touch to a playful day in summer. The scalloped
lace effect on the hem and sleeve is achieved because the soft, flexible Braid is so easy to handle. Added
details on the hat's brim give a wonderful finishing touch to the Summer Patchwork Girl.

YOU WILL NEED

- 25.5 x 28cm (10 x 11in) piece pale blue 24 count Congress Cloth (Zweigart 9406/594)
- Kreinik Very Fine (#4) Braid 003 Red
- Kreinik Fine (#8) Braid 001HL Silver Hi-Lustre, 003 Red, 005HL Black Hi-Lustre
- Kreinik ⅛" Ribbon 091 Star Yellow
- Kreinik ¹⁄₁₆" Ribbon 2122 Curry
- Kreinik Cord 001C Silver, 051C Sapphire
- Kreinik Facets™ Silver (2 skeins), Sapphire
- Anchor/DMC stranded cotton (floss): 226/702, 228/700, 295/726
- Anchor/DMC No.8 pearl cotton: 2/White
- Anchor/DMC No.5 pearl cotton: 2/White, 290/444, 906/829, 433/996, 1012/754

1   Prepare your canvas and design outline as described in step1 Spring Patchwork Girl on page 91 (using Fig 2 on page 99).

To work the bonnet, dress, hand and shoe:

2   Begin stitching using No.5 pearl cotton 2/White to fill the bonnet crown with vertical straight stitches.

Fill the bonnet brim with Parisian stitch in horizontal rows using Fine (#8) Braid 003 to work the short stitches and No.5 pearl cotton 2/White to work the long stitches.

Fill the dress area with alternating stripes of horizontal gobelin stitch worked over five canvas threads in diagonal rows using No.5 pearl cotton 433/996, and upright 2 x 2 cross stitches worked with Fine (#8) Braid 003.

Use No.5 pearl cotton 1012/754 to fill the hand area with vertical straight stitches.

Use No.8 pearl cotton 2/White to fill the sock area with basketweave stitch, and Fine (#8) Braid 005HL to fill the shoe area with basketweave stitch.
Note: Do not add the bow to the bonnet or work the lace on the dress at this time.

To work the flower and grass:

3   Fill the centre of the flower with one large spider's web stitch, using No.5 pearl cotton 906/829 for the

spokes and weaving them with ¹⁄₁₆" Ribbon 2122.

Use ⅛" Ribbon 091 to work straight stitch petals, each approximately 1.25cm (½in) long, around the centre of the flower.

Use No.5 pearl cotton 290/444 to work a long, detached chain stitch (lazy daisy stitch) around each petal.

Use four strands of stranded cotton (floss) 226/702 to work the stem in horizontal gobelin stitch over four canvas threads.

Use four strands of stranded cotton (floss) 226/702 to work the leaves in leaf variation stitch, extending the stitch units to fit the individual leaf shapes. Work a long straight stitch down the centre of each leaf.

Use four strands of stranded cotton (floss) 228/700 to fill the grass area with random-length straight stitches (see photograph on page 93).

To work the bonnet bow and lace on the dress:

4   Use ⅛" Ribbon 091 to work a straight stitch band between the brim and crown of the bonnet. Cut another piece of Ribbon about 20cm (8in) long and tie it in a small bow. Use one strand of stranded cotton (floss) 295/726 to stitch it to the bonnet and tack down the loops and streamers, allowing them to pouf and billow gently. Trim the streamers to the desired length.

Trim the dress with Pekinese stitch 'lace' using Fine (#8) Braid 003 to work a single row of backstitches 3mm (⅛in) long along the bottom edge of the sleeve and the hem line of the dress and 60cm (24in) and 90cm (36in) lengths of red Very Fine (#4) Braid 003 for the loops.

To work the star panel:

5   Refer to step 5 of the Spring Patchwork Girl on page 92, and the star panel stitch diagram on page 92. Use Fine (#8) Braid 003 for the centres, No.5 pearl cotton 433/996 for the points, No.5 pearl cotton 2/White for the area around the stars and Fine (#8) Braid 001HL for the French knots in the star panel.

6   Refer to steps 6 and 7 of the Spring Patchwork Girl on page 92 for couching the star panel outline and the whole design outline using Silver and Sapphire Facets™ with Cord 001C and 051C. Frame when finished.

AUTUMN PATCHWORK GIRL

Variegated Ombre creates the right shade of autumn leaves that magically turn from

gold to yellow, to lime, orange and brown. The leaves are collected with a realistic rake of Gunmetal Braid.

The garnet metallic in the dress contrasts with the pearl cotton to give it visual play.

◆

YOU WILL NEED

- 25.5 x 28cm (10 x 11in) piece pale blue 24 count Congress Cloth (Zweigart 9406/594)
- Kreinik Fine (#8) Braid 001HL Silver Hi-Lustre
- Kreinik Tapestry (#12) Braid 080HL Garnet Hi-Lustre
- Kreinik Medium (#16) Braid 011HL Gunmetal Hi-Lustre
- Kreinik Ombre 1800 Misty Sunrise
- Kreinik Cord 001C Silver, 051C Sapphire
- Kreinik Facets™ Silver (2 skeins), Sapphire
- Anchor/DMC stranded cotton (floss): 215/320, 277/831, 295/726
- Anchor/DMC No.8 pearl cotton: 2/White, 403/310
- Anchor/DMC No.5 pearl cotton: 290/444, 333/900, 1012/754

1   Prepare your canvas and design outline as described in step1 Spring Patchwork Girl on page 91 (using Fig 3 on page 100).

To work the hat, dress, hand and boot:

2   Begin stitching by using one strand of stranded cotton (floss) 277/831 together with three strands of 295/726 to fill the hat crown and brim with double brick stitch. Work the hat brim in the direction opposite that of the crown.

Use Tapestry (#12) Braid 080HL to couch a line between the brim and crown of the hat, using the same Braid for the couching thread.

Fill the dress area with Hungarian diamonds, alternating diamonds of Tapestry (#12) Braid 080HL and No.5 pearl cotton 333/900. To define the sleeve on a garment, stitch its pattern in the direction opposite that of the coat or dress.

Use No.5 pearl cotton 1012/754 to fill the hand area with vertical straight stitches.

Use No.8 pearl cotton 403/310 to fill the boot area with basketweave stitch.

To work the rake, leaves and grass:

3   Use No.5 pearl cotton 290/444 to work three long, straight stitches for the rake handle.

Use Medium (#16) Braid 011HL to work straight stitches for the head of the rake, working the tines first,

then the crossbars (see the picture detail below).

Use Ombre 1800 to work scattered leaf variation stitches throughout the sky. Begin, stitch and end each leaf individually, taking special care to secure the beginning and ending tails. Do not travel from one leaf to another as this will show on the right side of the work. Tilt the leaves in alternating directions.

Use four strands of stranded cotton (floss) 215/320 to fill the grass area with random-length straight stitches.

To work the star panel:

4   Refer to step 5 of the Spring Patchwork Girl on page 92, and the star panel stitch diagram on page 92. Use Tapestry (#12) Braid 080HL for the centres, No.5 pearl cotton 333/900 for the points, No.8 pearl cotton 2/White for the area around the stars and Fine (#8) Braid 001HL for the French knots in the star panel.

5   Refer to steps 6 and 7 of the Spring Patchwork Girl on page 92 for couching the star panel outline and the whole design outline using Silver and Sapphire Facets™ with Cord 001C and 051C. Frame when finished.

WINTER PATCHWORK GIRL

Sparkling snowflakes fall against a background of an evergreen tree with long stitches of metallic thread to give a lightly textured look. The coat and hat accents are stitched in pearl Ombre creating a faux fur texture so popular in fashion and so easy to accomplish with French knots. With black Hi-Lustre boots and gold French knot buttons, Winter Patchwork Girl generates a frosty, crystallised and tactile effect.

◆

YOU WILL NEED

- 25.5 x 28cm (10 x 11in) piece of pale blue 24 count Congress Cloth (Zweigart 9406/594)
- Kreinik Blending Filament 031 Crimson
- Kreinik Very Fine (#4) Braid 009 Emerald
- Kreinik Fine (#8) Braid 001HL Silver Hi-Lustre, 005HL Black Hi-Lustre
- Kreinik Tapestry (#12) Braid 002 Gold
- Kreinik Ombre 3200 Solid Pearl
- Kreinik Cord 001C Silver, 051C Sapphire
- Kreinik Facets™ Silver (2 skeins), Sapphire
- Anchor/DMC stranded cotton (floss): 1006/304
- Anchor/DMC No.8 pearl cotton: 2/White
- Anchor/DMC No.5 pearl cotton: 218/890, 906/829, 1012/754

1   Prepare your canvas and design outline as described in step 1 Spring Patchwork Girl on page 91 (using Fig 4 on page 100).

To work the hat, coat, hand and boot:

2   Begin stitching by using one strand of Blending Filament 031 together with three strands of stranded cotton (floss) 1006/304 to fill the crown area of the hat and the coat with Parisian stitch. Stitch the hat in the same direction as the sleeve. To define the sleeve on a garment, stitch its pattern in the direction opposite that of the coat or dress. Do not work the coat buttons at this time.

Use Ombre 3200 to fill the hat brim, cuff and coat hem area with French knots, wrapping the needle once for each knot. Do not pack these areas too tightly with knots; leave one canvas thread bare on each side of each knot.

Use No.5 pearl cotton 1012/754 to fill the hand area with vertical straight stitches, tucking the stitches under the bottom row of French knots on the sleeve cuff.

Use Fine (#8) Braid 005HL to fill the boot area with basketweave stitch.

To work the tree, snow and snowflakes:

3   Use No.5 pearl cotton 218/890 to fill the tree area with stripes of horizontal gobelin stitch worked over five canvas threads in diagonal rows.

Use Very Fine (#4) Braid 009 to work a long straight stitch between the diagonal stripes of the tree.

Use No.5 pearl cotton 906/829 to fill the tree trunk area with brick stitch over four canvas threads.

Use Ombre 3200 to fill the ground area with random-length straight stitches. Make the surface of the snow smooth and flowing rather than spiked like the grass in the other embroideries.

Use Ombre 3200 to work scattered Rhodes stitch variation snowflakes throughout the sky. Begin, stitch and end each snowflake individually, taking special care to secure the beginning and ending tails. Do not travel from one snowflake to another as this will show on the right side of the work. Tiny dabs of washable glue may be helpful in securing tails.

To work the coat buttons:

4   Use Tapestry (#12) Braid 002 to work five French knot buttons along the edge of the coat, wrapping the needle twice for each knot.

To work the star panel:

5   Refer to step 5 of the Spring Patchwork Girl on page 92, and the star panel stitch diagram on page 92. Use one strand of Blending Filament 031 together with three strands of stranded cotton (floss) 1006/304 for the centres, No.5 pearl cotton 218/890 for the points, No.8 pearl cotton 2/White for the area around the stars and Fine (#8) Braid 001HL for the French knots in the star panel.

6   Refer to steps 6 and 7 of the Spring Patchwork Girl on page 92 for couching the star panel outline and the whole design outline using Silver and Sapphire Facets™ with Cord 001C and 051C. Frame when finished.

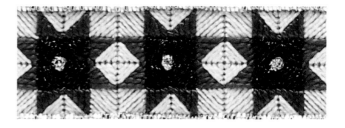

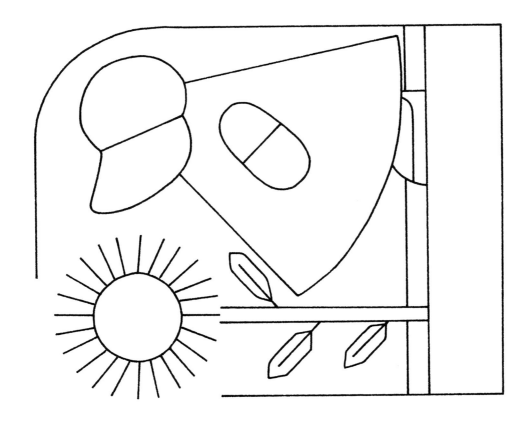

Fig 2 Summer Patchwork Girl - stitching outline

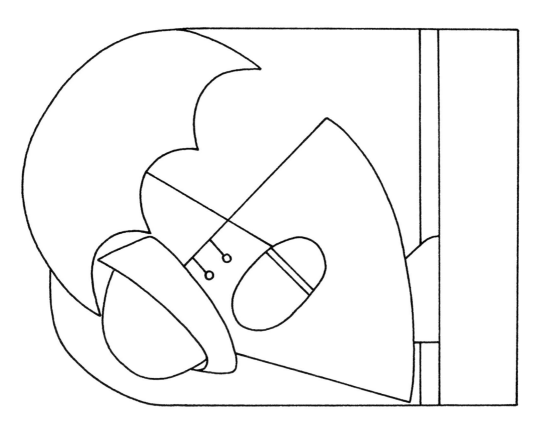

Fig 1 Spring Patchwork Girl - stitching outline

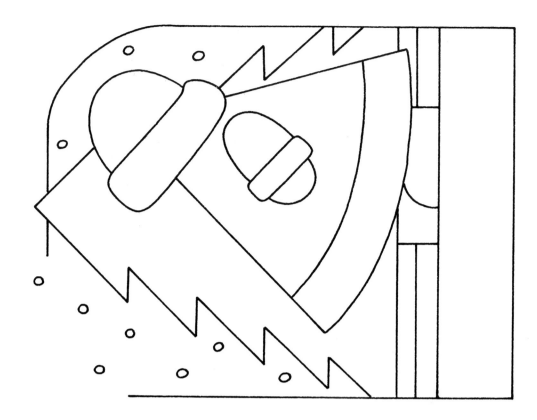

Fig 4 Winter Patchwork Girl - stitching outline

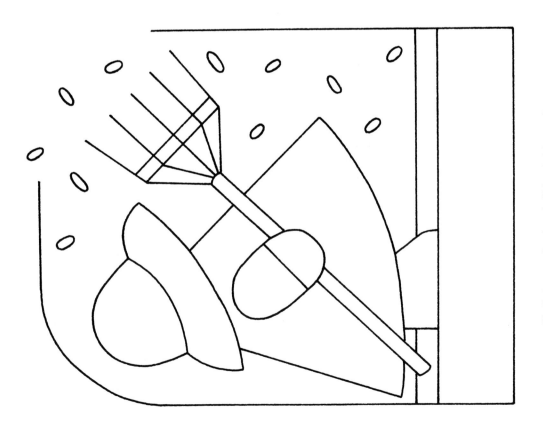

Fig 3 Autumn Patchwork Girl - stitching outline

FRIENDSHIP ANGEL

Designed by Sara Lee J. Allen, USA

THE FRIENDSHIP ANGEL IS THE PERFECT COMPANION. THE ILLUSION OF MOVEMENT AND

LIGHTNESS TO THE WINGS IS CREATED BY AN OPEN STITCH IN VERY FINE (#4) BRAID, TRANSFORMING

THE SOLID CANVAS WITH A SPIRITED SENSE OF PLAY.

WHITE FINE (#8) BRAID IS PERFECT FOR CREATING A TEXTURED AND DECORATIVE SHIMMERING

EFFECT ON THE APRON. THE VERY FINE (#4) BRAID USED IN THE DRESS CREATES A PATTERN OF DEFINITION

BY OUTLINING THE TRADITIONAL SCOTCH STITCH AND CREATES A SUBTLE LIGHT PLAY. KREINIK TORSADE

IS USED TO FRAME AND DEFINE THIS WHIMSICAL AND PROTECTIVE ANGEL.

Stitching Notes

Design Size: *126 stitches wide x 126 high*
Finished Size: *13.5 x 13.5cm (5¼ x 5 ¼in) approximately*
Each line on the stitching diagrams represents one canvas thread.

YOU WILL NEED

♦ 20 x 20cm (8 x 8in) piece of white 24 count Congress Cloth (Zweigart 9406/194)
♦ Anchor/DMC stranded cotton (floss) 43/815, 66/3688, 176/793, 360/839, 381/938, 941/792, 1021/761, 1026/225
♦ Black seed beads
♦ Kreinik Very Fine (#4) Braid 202HL Aztec Gold Hi-Lustre ·
♦ Kreinik Fine (#8) Braid 100 White
♦ Kreinik Torsade 2mm Gold, 2m (2yd)
♦ Underlining fabric (e.g. gold lamé)
♦ Backing fabric
♦ Sewing thread
♦ Wadding (batting)
♦ Polyester filling
♦ Heavy cardboard
♦ Sewing thread to match cording

'For a good angel will go with him,
his journey will be successful, and
he will come home safe and sound.'
BOOK OF ANGELS

1 First prepare your canvas by taping the edges to prevent them from raveling. Carefully centre the canvas over Fig 1 (the angel outline overleaf), making sure the bottom of the dress and apron are drawn on the straight grain of the canvas (in the ditch between two canvas threads) so the angel will stand up straight. You may need to adjust the canvas over the drawing, or adjust your drawn lines to accommodate this. Using a permanent marking pen, lightly trace the angel outline (wings, dress, head and apron). This is the back side.

2 From the back of the canvas, tack (baste) along the drawn lines with a medium colour sewing thread. This will allow you to stitch from the front and avoid having to cover heavy black lines with delicate and light threads or open stitch patterns. The tacking (basting) threads should only be removed when they are no longer needed to outline an area, and should be pulled out with care.

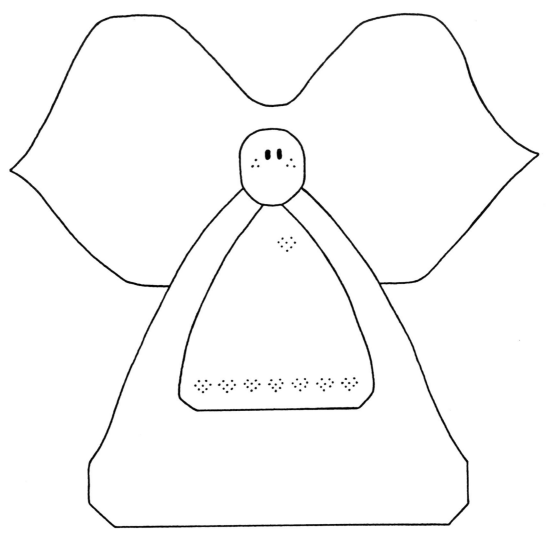

Fig 1 Angel outline

To work the face:

3   Following the stitch diagram for the face (right), begin stitching in basketweave stitch, using three strands of stranded cotton (floss) 1026/225. The tacked (basted) line for the face is only a guideline for placing the face in the right area: do not worry if the face diagram does not exactly fit within the guideline. Do not leave spaces for the eyes and freckles, these will be stitched over the top of the face stitches.

4   Using one strand of stranded cotton (floss) 1021/761, stitch French Knots for freckles (three on each cheek). Then attach one black seed bead for each eye

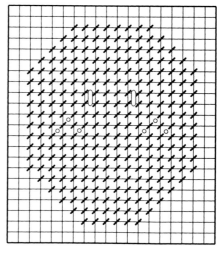

Stitch diagram – Face

where indicated on the diagram using a cross stitch in two strands of 1021/761. To attach a seed bead (see Fig 2), bring the needle up at A and thread a bead on the needle. Put the needle down at B, bring it up at C, slide the needle through the bead again and put the needle down at D. End thread tails under the stitching on the back.

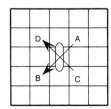

Fig 2 Attaching a bead

To work the wings:

5   Starting at the top centre (above the head), stitch the wings in mirror images, in woven stitch variation using Kreinik Very Fine (#4) Braid 202HL. This stitch is worked in vertical rows, with each stitch covering two intersections. No stitches share holes. Stitch the left wing from the centre to the left, and the right wing from the centre to the right, reversing the angle of the first rows of stitches – this will make the shaping of the wings match.

To work the apron:

6   Stitch the apron in horizontal rows of woven stitch, using Fine (#8) Braid 100 and following the tacked (basted) outline to shape the sides. Add the heart embellishments, using three strands of stranded cotton (floss) 43/815, by stitching the hearts over the top of the woven stitch pattern, using the open holes (see stitch diagram for the heart motif below). Make the three short vertical stitches, then cross them with a horizontal stitch. Lastly, place a cross stitch over the top as charted (Fig 3). Do not bury thread when travelling from heart to heart as this will show through on the front.

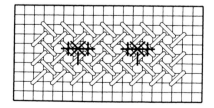

Stitch diagram – Heart Motif

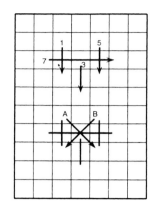

Fig 3 Working the heart motif

To work the dress:

7   Stitch the dress in horizontal rows of Scotch stitch, beginning directly below the apron (to avoid having to compensate), using three strands of stranded cotton (floss). With 43/815, work a row of Scotch stitches, skipping every four threads. With 176/793, fill in the gaps with Scotch stitches. The alternating rows are worked in 941/792 and 66/3688. Shape the dress around the apron and wings.

8   After all the Scotch stitches are complete, embellish the dress with Kreinik Very Fine (#4) Braid 202HL in a running stitch worked over and under two canvas threads, first vertically, then horizontally. The running stitches are centred between the blocks of Scotch stitches.

To work the hair:

9   Work the hair using stranded cotton (floss) – two strands each of 360/839 and 381/938 together in the needle. Following the stitch diagram for the head, stitch three rows of outline stitches along the top of the angel's head, from the top of one ear to the top of the other ear. The first row should share holes with the face stitches.

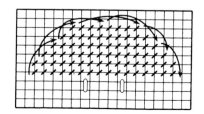

Stitch diagram – Head

Each stitch should be approximately four to five canvas threads long. At the top centre, make a short vertical stitch to create the effect of a centre parting in her hair. Do not finish off the thread yet.

10 Create the pigtails by using stranded cotton (floss) 360/839 and 381/938 together, cutting three 20cm (8in) lengths – two dark and one light. Separate the threads and use ten strands of dark and four strands of light. Tie an overhand knot in one end of the fourteen strands (close to the end). Holding the knotted end securely, tightly twist the 20cm (8in) length of thread until it almost begins to kink. Carefully fold the twisted thread in half, allowing the thread to twist back on itself. Tie another overhand knot in the ends of the twisted cord, just above the previous knot, then trim the ends of the threads evenly. Repeat for the second pigtail.

Tack (baste) the twisted cord pigtails in place above the angel's 'ears', stitching through the loop of the cord with the four-strand hair thread.

To finish the angel:

11 Place a piece of underlining fabric (gold nylon tricot lamé provides a nice background 'glow') face down on the back of the angel. Next, lay one or two layers of wadding (batting) on top of the underlining fabric. From the front side of the angel, tack (baste) all layers in place around the outline.

12 Place the backing fabric on the front side of the angel, right sides together. Stitch around the outline through all layers, leaving the bottom open for turning and stuffing. Trim away excess canvas and fabric. Clip in towards the seam and around the curves and/or points, then carefully turn right side out.

From the front, stitch through all layers following the line between the dress and wings and up around the angel's head. (Be careful not to stitch into her hair/ pigtails.) This step makes the figure distinct from the wings. Stuff the body with polyester filling or cotton balls for desired firmness (the firmer the better).

13 Cut a piece of heavy cardboard slightly smaller than

the shape and size of the bottom opening. Cut a piece of backing fabric the same shape as the cardboard, leaving a small 2cm (¾in) seam allowance. Cover the cardboard with the backing fabric and carefully glue down the seam allowance with fabric glue. Stitch the covered base to the bottom of the angel with small, invisible stitches.

14 Slipstitch Kreinik Torsades 2mm Gold along the wings – from the bottom of one wing, across the top, make a hanging loop and around the other wing (see picture detail above). Tuck the ends into the seams where the wings meet the dress. The second piece of Torsades is attached up one side, around the head forming the halo, down the other side and around the base, tucking the tails in the seams where you started. Your angel is now complete.

CELESTIAL MOBILE

Designed by Rosemarie S. Walter, USA

TURN OFF THE LIGHTS, SING A SWEET LULLABY AND ENTER THE PLAYFUL WORLD OF KREINIK

GLOW-IN-THE-DARK THREADS. AS THE MAN IN THE MOON WATCHES IN HIS COLOURFUL NIGHTCAP, CHUBBY STARS

DANCE AS THEY SUSPEND FROM A NIGHT SKY DOME. EACH SHINING STAR PROTECTS AND DELIGHTS YOUR LITTLE

ONES AS THEY EASE GENTLY INTO SLEEP. SIMPLY EXPOSE THE THREADS TO LIGHT AND WATCH AS THEY

'GLOW' FOR UP TO FIFTEEN MINUTES.

Stitching Notes

Dome: eight sections of 10 count plastic canvas, each 67
stitches high x 35 wide (at the base), measuring 9 x
17cm (3½ x 6¾in)

Moon: 44 stitches high x 29 wide, measuring 5 x 7.5cm
(2 x 3in) on 14 count plastic canvas

Stars: 47 stitches high x 50 wide, measuring 9 x 8.25cm
(3½ x 3¼in) on 14 count plastic canvas

*Each square on the charts represents one hole of the
plastic canvas.*

*Amounts of metallic threads refer to one reel unless
otherwise stated.*

YOU WILL NEED

- Two sheets of 21 x 28cm (8¼ x 11in) 10 count
  clear plastic canvas
- Two sheets of 21 x 28cm (8¼ x 11in) 14 count
  clear plastic canvas
- Kreinik Fine (#8) Braid: 051F Tangerine, 052F
  Grapefruit, 053F Lime, 054F Lemon-Lime,
  055F Watermelon
- Kreinik Medium (#16) Braid: 051F Tangerine, 052F
  Grapefruit (60m/65yd), 053F Lime, 054F Lemon-
  Lime (20m/22yd), 055F Watermelon
- Kreinik ⅛" Ribbon: 051F Tangerine, 052F Grapefruit,
  053F Lime, 054F Lemon-Lime (20m/22yd),
  055F Watermelon

- Worsted-weight yarn, dark blue 4-ply
- Anchor/DMC stranded cotton (floss): 2/White,
  87/3607, 99/552, 130/809, 187/958, 236/3799
- Anchor/DMC No.3 pearl cotton 1/White (2 skeins)
- Fabric for dome lining (slightly more than the
  10 count plastic canvas sizes)
- Fabric glue

1   Following the outlines of the three stitch diagrams
(on pages 109–111) cut eight dome shapes from the 10
count plastic canvas. Then cut two moon shapes and
eight star shapes from the 14 count plastic canvas.

To work the dome:

2   Following the dome stitch diagram, stitch each
dome shape with blue yarn in half cross stitch. (Note the
diagram shows only part of this stitching.) With one
strand of No.3 pearl cotton, half cross stitch, reverse half
cross stitch and straight stitch each scallop shape
according to the diagram. With Kreinik ⅛" Ribbon 054F
stitch moon crescents on each dome shape according to
the diagram. With Kreinik ⅛" Ribbon 052F and Medium
(#16) Braid in 052F stitch the stars on the dome. With
Medium (#16) Braid in 052F stitch the French knots.

3   Using the dome shape as a pattern cut eight pieces
of fabric with an additional 6mm (¼in) seam allowance.
Turn the edges of the fabric under and sew fabric to the

backs of each dome shape to cover all blue stitching. Do not line the scallops. Whipstitch the pieces together with worsted-weight yarn to form the dome and then overcast the top opening. Overcast the bottom edge of the scallops with the white No.3 pearl cotton.

To work the moon:

4   With Kreinik Medium (#16) Braid and stranded cotton (floss) use half cross stitch to stitch one moon shape with colours as on the moon stitch diagram. (Note that for clarity the diagram shows only part of the moon face stitching.) For the second moon shape, turn the piece in the opposite direction and use reverse half cross stitch. Use two strands of stranded cotton (floss) 236/3799 to backstitch the mouth and eyes on both faces.

Using ⅛" Ribbon couch lines on the hat in colours indicated on the diagram (see photograph too).

5   To make a tassel, cut one 10cm (4in) length of each colour stranded cotton (floss) and the ⅛" Ribbon used in the hat. Cut a 15cm (6in) length of 187/958 for wrapping. Gather all the threads together at one end, then fold in half over a pencil or thin tube (to keep the loops organised). Tightly wrap 187/958 several times around the threads to create the neck, tying off with a

knot. Fringe the tassel by using a needle to separate the fibres of each thread, then trim to an even length of about 2.5cm (1in). Whipstitch the moon shapes together with matching threads and colours, attaching the tassel to the hat tip while whipstitching.

To work the stars:

6   There are four stars altogether, each with a different coloured shirt. The stars are worked in half cross stitch and reverse half cross stitch – two stars for each colour combination using threads and colours according to the star stitch diagram and key on page 111.

Cross stitch the stars' shirt outlines and backstitch the nappy (diaper) pins with Fine (#8) Braids. Use stranded cotton (floss) 236/3799 to backstitch the nappy (diaper) outlines and face details and form French knots for the belly buttons and eyes.

Make the bows on the shirts with ⅛" Ribbon (matching the shirt outline colours). Cut a 10cm (4in) length, fold it into bows, tack (baste) in place and pull the ends of the bows to the back.

Use ⅛" Ribbon 054F for the hair. Insert the needle from the front to the back in the centre top hole of the star, leaving the tail end long enough to touch the eyebrows. Fringe the hair. Finally, whipstitch matching stars together using threads and colours to match.

To assemble the mobile:

7 Cut a 25cm (10in) length of white No.3 pearl cotton, fold it in half and thread the loose ends through the whipstitch at the first couching line on the moon's hat. Knot to secure, then run the ends of the thread to the inside piece. Knot again 4cm (1½in) from the folded loop for a hanger.

Cut two 30cm (12in) lengths of No.3 pearl cotton and thread through the whipstitching on the moon, 7.5cm (3in) diagonally from the top hanger. Even up all four ends and knot close to the moon. Thread each of the four loose ends into the dome top centre holes in every alternate dome section. Pull all the ends to the inside evenly and knot 5cm (2in) from the ends, trimming the excess.

Cut four 15cm (6in) lengths of white No.3 pearl cotton and thread one each through the centre top of each star's whipstitching. Tie a knot in the end of the thread, then pass the needle through the thread to secure. Attach the end of the thread to the dome, behind the centre scallop in every alternate panel in which the moon is not attached.

To finish your mobile, place fabric glue on all the knots and allow to dry before hanging in place.

MOON STITCH DIAGRAM

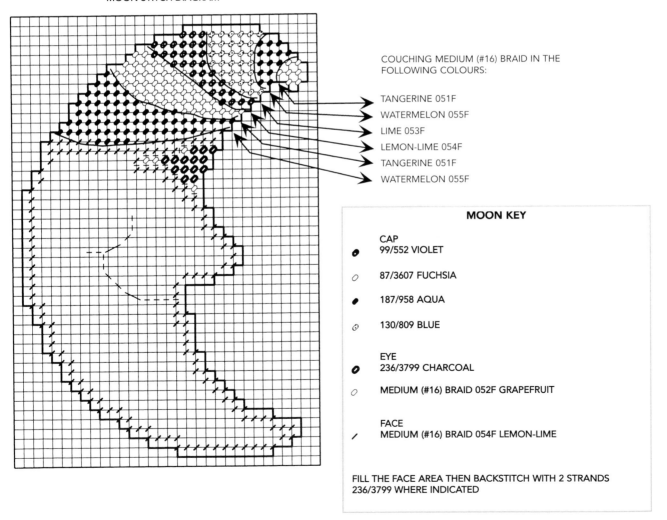

COUCHING MEDIUM (#16) BRAID IN THE FOLLOWING COLOURS:

TANGERINE 051F

WATERMELON 055F

LIME 053F

LEMON-LIME 054F

TANGERINE 051F

WATERMELON 055F

MOON KEY

CAP
99/552 VIOLET

87/3607 FUCHSIA

187/958 AQUA

130/809 BLUE

EYE
236/3799 CHARCOAL

MEDIUM (#16) BRAID 052F GRAPEFRUIT

FACE
MEDIUM (#16) BRAID 054F LEMON-LIME

FILL THE FACE AREA THEN BACKSTITCH WITH 2 STRANDS 236/3799 WHERE INDICATED

DOME STITCH DESIGN

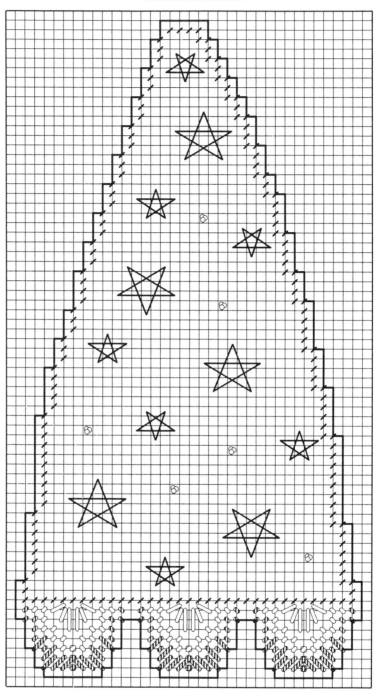

DOME KEY

 DARK BLUE WORSTED WEIGHT YARN –
FILL IN THE DOME AREA BEFORE STITCH-
ING THE STARS AND FRENCH KNOTS

 WHITE NO. 3 PEARL COTTON

KREINIK ⅛" RIBBON 054F LEMON-LIME

 KREINIK MEDIUM (#16) BRAID
052F GRAPEFRUIT

 KREINIK ⅛" RIBBON 052F
GRAPEFRUIT

STAR CHART

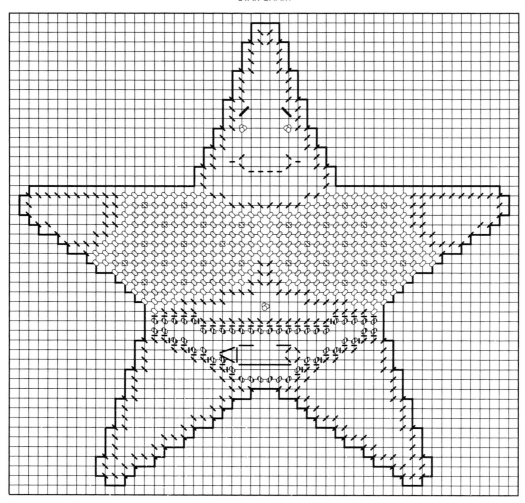

STAR KEY

/   KREINIK FINE (#8) BRAID 052F GRAPEFRUIT

⌀   WHITE NO. 3 PEARL COTTON

—   BACKSTITCH NAPPY OUTLINES AND FACE AND EYEBROW DETAILS 236/3799

⊗   EYES AND BELLY BUTTONS 236/3799

BODIES & FACES
FILL IN THE ARMS, LEGS, BELLIES AND HEAD AREAS WITH FINE (#8) BRAID 052F AS INDICATED ON THE DIAGRAM, THEN STITCH DETAILS ACCORDING TO INSTRUCTIONS.

		STAR 1	STAR 2	STAR 3	STAR 4
⌀ ⊗	SHIRT OUTLINE, CROSS STITCHES, & NAPPY PIN	FINE (#8) BRAID 055F WATERMELON	FINE (#8) BRAID 054F LEMON-LIME	FINE (#8) BRAID 053F LIME	FINE (#8) BRAID 051F TANGERINE
⌀	SHIRT MAIN COLOUR	130/809 BLUE	87/3607 PINK	99/552 VIOLET	187/958 GREEN

REGENCY STOCKING

Stocking cuff designed by
Anna-Marie Winter, Canada

THE RICHLY COLOURED WOODS AND GILDED
BRONZE APPLIQUÉS OF THE REGENCY PERIOD WERE
THE INSPIRATION FOR THIS DESIGN FOR A CHRISTMAS
STOCKING CUFF. ALTERNATIVELY IT COULD BE MADE
INTO A GLITTERING EVENING BAG. THE SUBTLE
REFLECTIVE QUALITIES OF SILK MORI® AND METALLIC
CORD, WORKED IN A DARK GARNET REMINISCENT OF
THE DEEP LUSTRE OF MAHOGANY, FORM THE BODY OF
THE CUFF. A MAGNIFICENT EDGING OF TORSADE,
JAPAN GOLD, METALLIC THREADS AND BEADS BORDERS
THE CUFF, ADDING ELEGANCE AND DRAMA TO A
DESIGN RICH IN COLOUR AND TEXTURE.
THREE WEIGHTS OF METALLIC THREAD AND TWO
SIZES OF TORSADE ARE USED IN THIS DESIGN TO ADD
SPARKLE AND HIGHLIGHTS TO THE BANDS. MEDIUM
(#16) BRAID IS COUCHED ALONG THE INSIDE OF THE
BAND AND IS USED TO MAKE A TWISTED CORD TO
OUTLINE THE BORDER OF THE CUFF. VERY FINE (#4)
BRAID IS USED TO LAY THE LATTICE PATTERN IN THE
BODY OF THE CUFF AND A FINE METALLIC CORD IS
USED TO HIGHLIGHT THE SILK STITCHES AND TO
COUCH THE METAL THREADS TO THE SURFACE OF THE
CANVAS. NOTE: INSTRUCTIONS ARE NOT GIVEN FOR
MAKING THE MAIN BODY OF THE STOCKING.

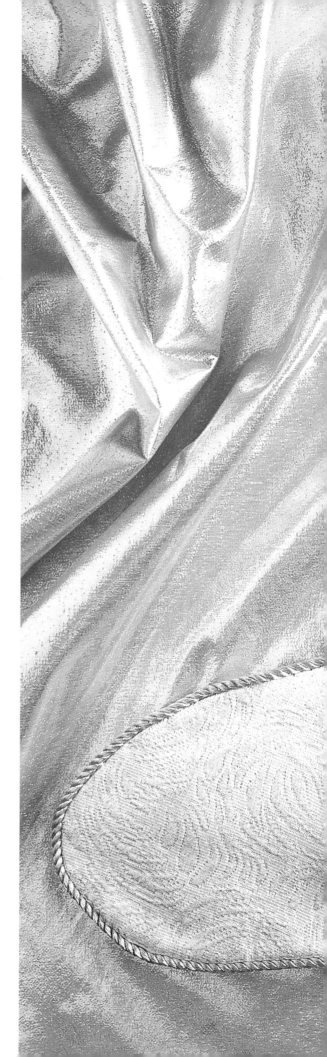

Stitching Notes

Stitch Count: 108 stitches wide x 73 high
Finished Cuff Size: 15 x 10cm (6 x 4in)
Each line on the chart represents one canvas thread.
Use straight stitch to couch the Japan Gold, and a
slanted stitch to couch the Torsade. Finish cut ends of
Japan Gold and Torsade by plunging through to the
reverse of the canvas, finishing the ends for each
section before another section is begun.

YOU WILL NEED

- 23 x 30cm (9 x 12in) piece of 18 count eggshell mono deluxe canvas
- Kreinik Silk Mori® 1119 Garnet, 35m (38yd)
- Kreinik Medium (#16) Braid: 080HL Garnet Hi-Lustre, 002J Gold
- Kreinik Very Fine (#4) Braid 002J Gold
- Kreinik Cord 080C Garnet
- Kreinik #1 Japan Gold 002J
- Kreinik #7 Japan Gold 002J
- Gold Torsade 1.5mm, 1m (1yd)
- Gold Torsade 1mm, 0.5m (½yd)
- Silk Couching Thread, Gold
- Gold seed beads size 11, 2 packets
- Beading thread or monocord
- Beeswax
- 23 x 25cm (9 x 12in) stretcher bars

1 Begin by placing the canvas on top of the stocking pattern given in Fig 1, positioning the canvas so as to leave approximately 4cm (1½in) all around the design. Align the straight lines of the design to the grain of the canvas threads, making sure that the top horizontal and side vertical lines follow one single canvas thread. Using a fine line permanent needlepoint marker, mark the top horizontal edge of the design by counting across 108 canvas threads. Mark the sides by counting down 73 threads on either side. Then trace the bottom scallop of the design on to the canvas.

2 Attach the canvas to the stretcher bars with tacks or staples no less than 1.25cm (½in) apart, making sure that the canvas is taut. A roller frame is not recommended for this design.

THE CUFF BORDER:

The bottom edge of the cuff is worked in a series of bands of different combinations of metallic threads and/or beads. All bands must begin and end between the same two pairs of vertical canvas threads to maintain a straight edge for finishing. Each band should fit snugly together with no canvas showing between the rows. Position the canvas so the scalloped edge of the cuff is at the top and the straight edge at the bottom. Work the bands in consecutive rows from right to left, one below the other. Begin the couching and beading threads by working a few small backstitches just inside

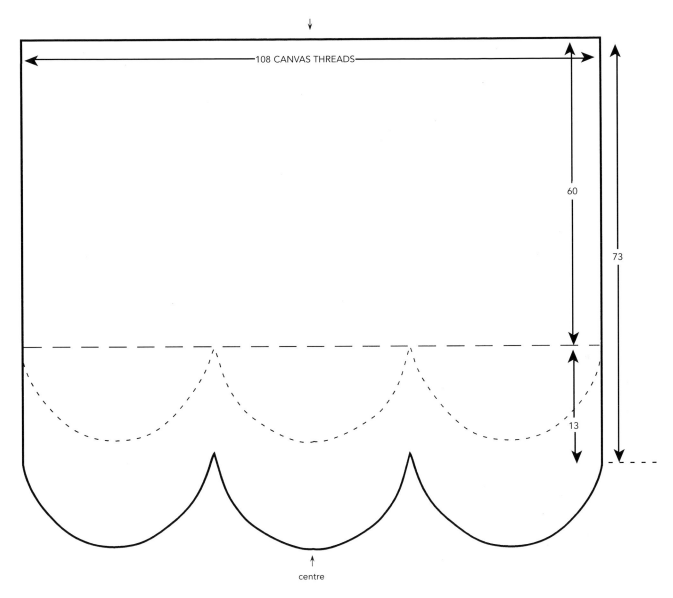

Fig 1 Stocking pattern

the design area. These backstitches will be covered as the bands are completed.

To work Band A:

3   A row of self-made, two-colour twisted cord forms Band A, the bottom wavy edge of the cuff. To make the twisted cord, cut 1m (1yd) lengths of Medium (#16) Braid in colours 002J and 080HL. Fold each length in half, slipping one colour through the other at the fold as shown in Fig 2. Knot the ends and begin twisting the cord either by hand or with a cording drill. When the desired twist is achieved, pinch the cord at the fold and bring the two knotted ends together, keeping the thread taut so

that it does not kink. Once the knots are joined, release the fold a few inches at a time to allow the cord to form a natural twist. When the cord is smoothly twisted to the end, tie all the ends into one knot.

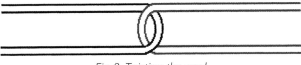

Fig 2 Twisting the cord

4   Working with the continuous length of twisted cord, begin at the top right edge of the cuff and lay the cord directly on the drawn line, leaving a tail of approximately 2.5cm (1in) extending beyond the cuff. Using a sharp crewel needle and a single strand of couching silk, begin couching the cord into place along the curved edges of the scallops, carefully maintaining the twist of the cord as you stitch. Place the couching stitches along every other groove of the twist, sinking it invisibly into the twist. Follow the curve and turn carefully at the points. Insert a large tapestry needle into the canvas at the point of the scallop and bend the cord around it to create a sharp point. Remove the tapestry needle and continue couching around the point. The point of each scallop should fall between the same two horizontal canvas threads. When the opposite edge of the cuff has been reached, work the couching thread over the last three twists and anchor it securely. Plunge the ends of the twisted cord through to the reverse side of the canvas. Take care that the ends are plunged between the same two horizontal canvas threads at either side.

To work Band B:

5   Band B is made up of rows of Japan Gold #7 and 1mm Torsade placed in the following order: three rows of Japan Gold #7, one row of Torsade, and one row of Japan Gold #7 (see Fig 3).

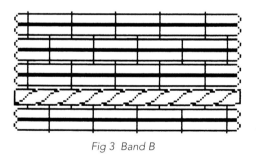

Fig 3 Band B

Open the skein of Japan Gold #7 and undo the knot holding the two ends together. Take the two ends and gently ease the pair of threads away from the skein. These will form the pairs of threads that will be couched. In this band each scallop is worked separately to maintain the point. Begin by couching a pair of Japan Gold #7 threads directly under the row of twisted cord using a crewel needle and a single strand of #1 Japan 002J. Leaving a 2.5cm (1in) tail, work the first scallop by couching the pair of threads directly under the row of twisted cord, beginning at the left edge and ending at

the first point. When the first point is reached, cut the Japan Gold #7, leaving a 2.5cm (1in) tail. Plunge the tail to the reverse side, directly above the point formed by the twisted cord. Secure the ends.

Work the second scallop in the same manner, this time beginning and ending the Japan Gold #7 at the points. Secure the ends before beginning the final scallop. Work the remaining scallop, beginning at the point and ending at the left edge of the cuff. Couch the remaining two pairs of Japan Gold #7 threads directly underneath in the same manner.

Couch a row of 1mm Torsade directly under the rows of Japan Gold #7, carefully turning at the points. Using a crewel needle and a single strand of couching silk, work in a continuous motion, beginning and ending at the edges of the cuff.

Complete Band B by couching a single pair of Japan Gold #7 threads directly under the Torsade. Work in a continuous motion, turning carefully, but not plunging at the points.

To work Band C:

6   Band C is composed of a single row of gold seed beads. Thread a beading needle with a long length of beading thread or monocord. You will be working with two needles and two lengths of monocord. Begin by anchoring the first length of monocord along the right edge of the cuff. String enough beads on the monocord to cover the distance halfway across the cuff. Temporarily anchor this thread by wrapping it around a tack on your frame.

Thread the second crewel needle with monocord and anchor it to the canvas at the right edge of the cuff. Using this thread, couch the row of beads into place, stitching between every two beads. Use one hand to gently push the beads together while couching them into place with your other hand, easing the beads around the points.

Continue working around the scallops to the left edge of the cuff, adding more beads as required. Take the last couching stitch four or five beads from the point. Bring the needle to the surface of the canvas, temporarily placing it out of the way. Release the first length of monocord from the tack and sink it along the left edge. Using the same thread and working backward toward the last stitch, couch the last four or five beads into place, stitching between each one. When you reach the first couching thread, sink both threads to the reverse side of the canvas, each on opposite sides of the bead. Remove the needles and tie the two threads together with several knots.

To work Band D:

7 Band D is composed of four rows of couched Medium (#16) Braid 002J and a single row of 1.5mm Torsade (Fig 4a).

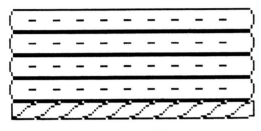

Fig 4a Band D

Thread a long length of Medium (#16) Braid 002J on a No.22 tapestry needle and anchor securely at the right edge. Using a crewel needle and a single strand of #1 Japan Thread 002J, couch into place directly below the row of beads. Use short running stitches and work through the centre of the Medium (#16) Braid (Fig 4b).

Fig 4b Band D

When you reach the left edge of the cuff, sink the Medium (#16) Braid to the reverse side of the canvas, bringing it back up to the left side (see Fig 4b). Continue couching this second row into place, this time working from left to right. When you reach the right edge, anchor securely in place on the reverse side.

Couch a row of 1.5 mm Torsade directly under the rows of Medium (#16) Braid, using the same method as in Band B. Complete the band by couching another

double row of Medium (#16) Braid directly under the row of Torsade.

To work Band E:

8 Band E is another row of gold seed beads couched into place directly under the previous row using the same method as in Band C.

THE CUFF BODY:

The body of the cuff is composed of alternating rows of reverse satin stitch blocks. When completed, these blocks are overstitched to form two very distinctive patterns – a subtle diamond pattern, and a highly textured beaded trellis pattern. The alternating direction of the stitches used in both the block and the diamond patterns allows the light to reflect differently from the silk to produce a shaded effect.

To work the base stitches:

9 Using four single strands of Silk Mori® 1119, a No.24 tapestry needle and a laying tool, begin working the background, filling the area of the cuff with reverse satin stitch blocks. Turn the canvas so the border is now along the bottom edge. Beginning at the top right corner, work the first row of reverse satin stitch blocks as illustrated in Fig 5 overleaf, working from right to left across the row. The first stitch must slant from bottom left to top right covering one canvas intersection. Eighteen blocks are required to complete the first row. Take care to lay the stitches as smoothly and evenly as possible. In addition to producing a shaded effect, the satin stitch blocks act as a base for a second layer of stitches. Work with a slightly tighter tension than normal to keep the holes between the stitches a bit more open, making it easier to work the overstitched pattern.

Work the second row directly under the row above, making sure each block alternates in direction. Ten complete, uncompensated rows are required before the satin stitch blocks need to be compensated along the scalloped border. Work the stitches right up to the beaded edge of Band E, compensating where necessary. Any uneven stitches or bare canvas will be covered by Band F later.

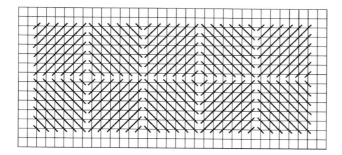

Fig 5 Reverse satin stitch blocks

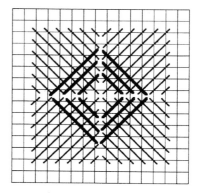

Fig 6 The primary diamond pattern

To work the primary diamond pattern:

10 This runs across the body of the cuff and is worked using two single strands of Silk Mori® 1119, a No.24 tapestry needle and a laying tool. Begin at the top right and work three diagonal stitches covering two, three and four canvas intersections over the corner of the satin stitch block. These three stitches will slant in the opposite direction to the stitches of the satin stitch block as shown in Fig 6.

Work the remaining sides of the diamond in the same manner, beginning with the shortest stitch and ending with the longest. Overstitch the remaining blocks with the primary diamond pattern. Odd numbered rows

will contain nine full diamond shapes; even numbered rows will contain eight completed diamond shapes plus two halves along each edge. You will need to compensate around the curves of the scallop.

To work the secondary diamond pattern:

11 When the primary pattern has been established, the secondary pattern of diamond shapes can be added. Using a single strand of Cord 080C and a No.26 tapestry needle, begin the pattern as shown in Fig 7, working in horizontal rows. Each primary diamond is

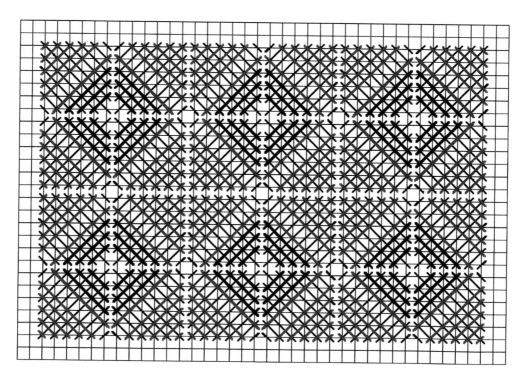

Fig 7 The secondary diamond pattern

outlined with a single line of cord. The spaces in between are filled with a secondary diamond pattern composed of one, two, three, four and five stitches in each quadrant.

To work the lattice pattern:

12 Once the primary and secondary diamond patterns have been completed, a lattice pattern, worked in a single strand of Very Fine (#4) Braid 002J, is laid across the surface of the reverse satin stitch blocks using a No.24 tapestry needle. Using long lengths of thread, begin at the top right corner, inserting the stitches into the corners of the blocks. Work all the stitches in one direction before crossing the threads in the opposite direction (Fig 8). (For clarity, the diagram doesn't show the previously worked stitches, only the outline of the blocks.)

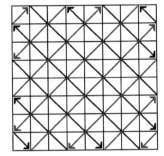

Fig 8 The lattice pattern

13 Once the lattice pattern has been completed in both directions, the intersections are secured with beads. Using a crewel needle and a long length of gold couching silk (run through a block of beeswax), attach three gold seed beads at each intersection, working in horizontal rows across the body of the cuff (Fig 9).

14 Complete the cuff embroidery by stitching Band F. This final band is a single couched row of 1.5mm Torsade worked after the stitching in the body of the cuff has been completed. The Torsade in this band sits directly over the top of the stitches forming the reverse satin blocks, covering any canvas that may show through where the body and scalloped edge of the cuff join.

15 The cuff can now be attached to a stocking of your choice. The one in the photograph was made from a metre (yard) of ivory brocade fabric, trimmed with 1.5m (1½yd) of 4mm Kreinik Gold Torsade.

16 To make two 18cm (7in) tassels follow step 5 on page 86 but use garnet Silk Mori® and gold Medium (#6) Braid for a wrapping. Once the tassels are made, stitch them to the cuff.

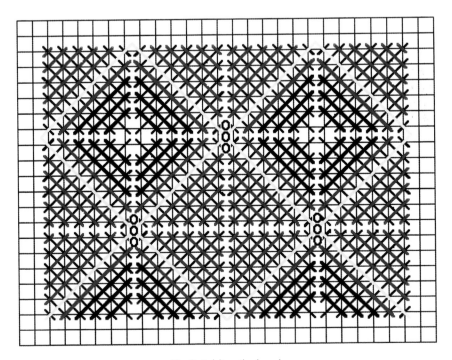

Fig 9 Adding the beads

KREINIK METALLIC THREAD COLOUR CHART

001 SILVER	009 EMERALD	019 PEWTER	033 ROYAL BLUE	085 PEACOCK	193 PALE MAUVE
001HL SILVER HI LUSTRE	009HL EMERALD HI LUSTRE	021 COPPER	034 CONFETTI	091 STAR YELLOW	194 PALE BLUE
002 GOLD	010HL STEEL GREY	021HL COPPER HI LUSTRE	041 CONFETTI PINK	092 STAR PINK	195 SUNBURST
002HL GOLD HI LUSTRE	011HL GUN METAL	022 BROWN	042 CONFETTI FUCHSIA	093 STAR MAUVE	198 PALE GREEN
003 RED	012 PURPLE	023 LILAC	043 CONFETTI GREEN	094 STAR BLUE	202HL AZTEC GOLD HI LUSTRE
003HL RED HI LUSTRE	012HL PURPLE HI LUSTRE	024 FUCHSIA	044 CONFETTI BLUE	095 STARBURST	203 FLAME
005 BLACK	013 BEIGE	024HL FUCHSIA HI LUSTRE	045 CONFETTI GOLD	100 WHITE	210 GOLD DUST
005HL BLACK HI LUSTRE	014 SKY BLUE	025 GREY	051HL SAPPHIRE HI LUSTRE	100 WHITE HI LUSTRE	212 GOLDEN SAND
006 BLUE	014HL SKY BLUE HI LUSTRE	026 AMETHYST	052HL BRONZE HI LUSTRE	101 PLATINUM	221 ANTIQUE GOLD
006HL BLUE HI LUSTRE	015 CHARTREUSE	027 ORANGE	060 MIDNIGHT	102 VATICAN GOLD	238 CHRISTMAS
007 PINK	015HL CHARTREUSE HI LUSTRE	028 CITRON	061 RUBY	102HL VATICAN GOLD HI LUSTRE	242HL MAGENTA SUNSET
007HL PINK HI LUSTRE	017HL WHITE GOLD HI LUSTRE	029 TURQUOISE	070 MARDI GRAS	127 YELLOW ORANGE	271 PLUM
008 GREEN	018 NAVY	031 CRIMSON	071 MISTY GOLD	191 PALE YELLOW	273 RED ORANGE
008HL GREEN HI LUSTRE	018HL NAVY HI LUSTRE	032 PEARL	080HL GARNET HI LUSTRE	192 PALE PINK	307 DEEP CORAL

CARE: Kreinik Blending Filament, Cord, Cable, Braids, Ribbons and Ombre are hand and machine washable and dry-cleanable. Do not use bleach. When ironing a finished piece containing Kreinik metallics, do not iron directly on the metallic thread.

KREINIK METALLIC THREAD COLOUR CHART

308 COLONIAL RED	2094HL HEATHER	026V VINTAGE AMETHYST	021J JAPAN COPPER	001C SILVER CORD	102C VATICAN GOLD CORD
326 HIBISCUS	2122 CURRY	150V VINTAGE AMBER	321J DARK JAPAN GOLD	002C GOLD CORD	104C COLONIAL GOLD CORD
329 BAHAMA BLUE	2829 SEAFOAM	152V VINTAGE SIENNA	1000 SOLID SILVER	003C RED CORD	105C ANTIQUE SILVER CORD
332 CANDY CANE	4639 LIGHT AQUA	153V VINTAGE BURGUNDY	1100 MISTY LIME	005C BLACK CORD	201C CHOCOLATE CORD
339 TROPICAL TEAL	5982 FOREST GREEN	154V VINTAGE VERDIGRIS	1200 MISTY APRICOT	007C PINK CORD	202C INDIGO CORD
393 SILVER NIGHT	9100 SUNLIGHT	051F TANGERINE	1300 MISTY VIOLET	008C GREEN CORD	205C ANTIQUE GOLD CORD
622 WEDGE-WOOD BLUE	9192 LIGHT PEACH	052F GRAPEFRUIT	1400 MISTY SCARLET	011C NICKEL CORD	208C WINE CORD
664 MAGENTA BLUE	9194 STAR GREEN	053F LIME	1500 MISTY RAINBOW	012C PURPLE CORD	209C CARNIVAL CORD
684 AQUA-MARINE	9200 BLOSSOM	054F LEMON-LIME	1600 MISTY LAVENDER	021C COPPER CORD	215C ANTIQUE COPPER CORD
713 PINK MAUVE	9294 PERIWINKLE	055F WATER-MELON	1700 MISTY GOLD	032C PEARL CORD	225C SLATE CORD
829 MINT JULEP	9300 ORCHID	001P SILVER CABLE	1800 MISTY SUNRISE	034C CONFETTI CORD	
850 MALLARD	9400 BABY BLUE	002P GOLD CABLE	1900 MISTY SUNSET	041C CONFETTI PINK CORD	*Actual colours may vary slightly from picture*
1223 PASSION PLUM	002V VINTAGE GOLD	001J JAPAN SILVER	2000 SOLID GOLD	051C SAPPHIRE CORD	
1432 BLUE ICE	003V VINTAGE RED	002J JAPAN GOLD	3200 SOLID PEARL	080C GARNET CORD	

Use a press cloth on reverse side, then iron. Do not use steam. Blending Filament, Cord, Cable, Braids and Ribbons can be tumble dried on low setting. Japan Threads are dry cleanable only.

KREINIK THREAD COLOUR REFERENCE CHART

KEY (* *denotes colour availability*)

- BF = Blending Filament
- FN = Fine (#8) Braid
- MD = Medium (#16) Braid
- 1/8 = 1/8" Ribbon
- 1 Ply = Cord
- VF = Very Fine (#4)
- TP = Tapestry™ (#12)
- HY = Heavy (#32) Braid
- 1/16 = 1/16" Ribbon

#	Name	BF	VF	FN	TP	MD	HY	1/8	1/16
001	Silver	*	*	*	*	*	*	*	*
001HL	Silver Hi Lustre	*	*	*	*	*	*	*	*
002	Gold	*	*	*	*	*	*	*	*
002HL	Gold Hi Lustre	*	*	*	*	*	*	*	*
003	Red	*	*	*	*	*	*	*	*
003HL	Red Hi Lustre	*	*	*	*	*	*	*	*
005	Black	*	*	*	*	*	*	*	*
005HL	Black Hi Lustre	*		*		*	*	*	*
006	Blue	*	*	*		*	*	*	*
006HL	Blue Hi Lustre	*							
007	Pink	*	*	*	*	*	*	*	*
007HL	Pink Hi Lustre	*		*		*	*	*	*
008	Green	*	*	*		*	*	*	*
008HL	Green Hi Lustre	*		*	*	*	*	*	*
009	Emerald	*	*	*	*	*	*	*	*
009HL	Emerald Hi Lustre	*	*	*	*	*	*	*	*
010HL	Steel Grey	*		*	*	*	*	*	*
011HL	Gun Metal	*		*		*	*	*	*
012	Purple	*	*	*	*	*	*	*	*
012HL	Purple Hi Lustre	*		*		*	*	*	*
013	Beige	*	*	*	*	*	*	*	*
014	Sky Blue	*	*	*		*	*	*	*
014HL	Sky Blue Hi Lustre	*		*	*	*	*	*	*
015	Chartreuse	*	*	*	*	*	*	*	*
015HL	Chartreuse Hi Lustre	*		*	*	*	*	*	*
017HL	White Gold Hi Lustre			*		*	*	*	*
018	Navy	*	*	*		*	*	*	*
018HL	Navy Hi Lustre	*		*	*	*	*	*	*
019	Pewter	*		*	*	*	*	*	*
021	Copper	*	*	*		*	*	*	*
021HL	Copper Hi Lustre	*		*	*	*	*	*	*
022	Brown	*	*	*		*	*	*	*
023	Lilac	*	*	*		*	*	*	*
024	Fuchsia	*	*	*	*	*	*	*	*
024HL	Fuchsia Hi Lustre	*		*		*	*	*	*
025	Grey	*	*	*	*	*	*	*	*
026	Amethyst	*	*	*	*	*	*	*	*
027	Orange	*	*	*	*	*	*	*	*
028	Citron	*	*	*	*	*	*	*	*
029	Turquoise	*	*	*	*	*	*	*	*
031	Crimson	*	*	*	*	*	*	*	*
032	Pearl	*	*	*	*	*	*	*	*
033	Royal Blue	*	*	*	*	*	*	*	*
034	Confetti	*		*		*	*	*	*
041	Confetti Pink	*	*	*		*	*	*	*
042	Confetti Fuchsia	*	*	*		*	*	*	*
043	Confetti Green	*		*		*	*	*	*
044	Confetti Blue	*				*	*	*	*
045	Confetti Gold	*				*	*	*	*
051HL	Sapphire Hi Lustre	*		*	*	*	*	*	*
052HL	Bronze	*		*	*	*	*	*	*
060	Midnight	*	*	*		*	*	*	*
061	Ruby	*	*	*		*	*	*	*
070	Mardi Gras			*		*	*	*	*
071	Misty Gold			*		*	*	*	*
080HL	Garnet Hi Lustre	*		*		*	*	*	*
085	Peacock	*	*	*		*	*	*	*
091	Star Yellow	*	*	*		*	*	*	*
092	Star Pink	*	*	*		*	*	*	*
093	Star Mauve	*	*	*		*	*	*	*
094	Star Blue	*	*	*		*	*	*	*
095	Starburst	*	*	*		*	*	*	*
100	White	*	*	*	*	*	*	*	*
100HL	White Hi Lustre	*		*		*	*	*	*
101	Platinum		*	*	*	*	*	*	*

#	Name	BF	VF	FN	TP	MD	HY	1/8	1/16
102	Vatican Gold		*	*	*	*	*	*	*
102HL	Vatican Gold Hi Lustre		*		*	*	*	*	*
127	Yellow Orange			*		*	*	*	*
191	Pale Yellow		*	*	*	*	*	*	*
192	Pale Pink		*	*		*	*	*	*
193	Pale Mauve		*			*	*	*	*
194	Pale Blue		*	*		*	*	*	*
195	Sunburst		*			*	*	*	*
198	Pale Green		*	*		*	*	*	*
202HL	Aztec Gold Hi Lustre		*	*	*	*	*	*	*
203	Flame		*			*	*	*	*
210	Gold Dust		*	*	*		*	*	*
212	Golden Sand		*	*		*	*	*	*
221	Antique Gold		*	*	*	*	*	*	*
238	Christmas		*			*	*	*	*
242HL	Magenta Sunset		*	*		*	*	*	*
271	Plum		*			*	*	*	*
273	Red Orange		*			*	*	*	*
307	Deep Coral		*			*	*	*	*
308	Colonial Red		*	*		*	*	*	*
326	Hibiscus		*	*	*	*	*	*	*
329	Bahama Blue		*	*	*	*	*	*	*
332	Candy Cane		*			*	*	*	*
339	Tropical Teal		*			*	*	*	*
393	Silver Night		*			*	*	*	*
622	Wedgewood Blue		*			*	*	*	*
664	Magenta Blue		*	*	*	*	*	*	*
684	Aquamarine		*	*	*	*	*	*	*
713	Pink Mauve		*			*	*	*	*
829	Mint Julep		*			*	*	*	*
850	Mallard		*	*	*	*	*	*	*
1223	Passion Plum		*	*		*	*	*	*
1432	Blue Ice		*	*	*	*	*	*	*
2094HL	Heather		*	*		*	*	*	*
2122	Curry		*	*		*	*	*	*
2829	Seafoam		*			*	*	*	*
4639	Light Aqua		*			*	*	*	*
5982	Forest Green		*	*	*	*	*	*	*
9100	Sunlight		*	*		*	*	*	*
9192	Light Peach		*	*	*	*	*	*	*
9194	Star Green		*	*	*	*	*	*	*
9200	Blossom		*	*		*	*	*	*
9294	Periwinkle		*	*	*	*	*	*	*
9300	Orchid		*	*	*	*	*	*	*
9400	Baby Blue		*	*	*	*	*	*	*

GLOW-IN-THE-DARK

#	Name	BF	VF	FN	TP	MD	HY	1/8	1/16
051F	Tangerine	*	*	*		*	*	*	*
052F	Grapefruit	*	*	*		*	*	*	*
053F	Lime	*	*	*		*	*	*	*
054F	Lemon-Lime	*	*	*		*	*	*	*
055F	Watermelon	*	*	*		*	*.	*	*

VINTAGE

#	Name	BF	VF	FN	TP	MD	HY	1/8	1/16
002V	Vintage Gold	*	*	*	*	*		*	*
003V	Vintage Red	*	*	*	*	*		*	*
026V	Vintage Amethyst	*	*	*	*	*		*	*
150V	Vintage Amber	*	*	*	*	*		*	*
152V	Vintage Sienna	*	*	*	*	*		*	*
153V	Vintage Burgundy	*	*	*	*	*		*	*
154V	Vintage Verdigris	*	*	*	*	*		*	*

CORD

#	Name	1Ply	VF	FN	TP	MD	HY	1/8	1/16
001C	Silver	*	*	*		*		*	*
002C	Gold	*	*	*		*		*	*
003C	Red	*		*		*		*	*
005C	Black	*		*		*		*	*
007C	Pink	*		*		*		*	*
008C	Green	*		*		*		*	*
011C	Nickel	*		*		*		*	*
012C	Purple	*		*		*		*	*
021C	Copper	*		*		*		*	*

KREINIK THREAD COLOUR REFERENCE CHART

CORD		1ply	VF	FN	TP	MD	HY	1/8	1/16
032C	Pearl	*		*		*		*	*
034C	Confetti	*		*		*		*	*
041C	Confetti Pink	*		*		*		*	*
051C	Sapphire	*		*		*		*	*
080C	Garnet	*		*		*		*	*
102C	Vatican Gold	*	*	*	*	*		*	*
104C	Colonial Gold	*		*		*		*	*
105C	Antique Silver	*		*		*		*	*
201C	Chocolate	*		*		*		*	*
202C	Indigo	*		*		*		*	*
205C	Antique Gold	*	*	*	*	*		*	*
208C	Wine	*		*		*		*	*
209C	Carnival	*		*		*		*	*
215C	Antique Copper	*	*	*		*		*	*
225C	Slate	*		*		*		*	*

JAPAN THREAD		#1	#5	#7	VF	FN	TP	MD	1/8	1/16
001J	Silver	*	*	*	*	*	*	*	*	*
002J	Gold	*	*	*	*	*	*	*	*	*
021J	Copper			*						
321J	Dark Gold	*				*	*	*	*	*

OMBRE		
1000	Solid Silver	*
1100	Misty Lime	*
1200	Misty Apricot	*
1300	Misty Violet	*
1400	Misty Scarlet	*
1500	Misty Rainbow	*
1600	Misty	*
1700	Lavender	*
1800	Misty Gold	*
1900	Misty Sunrise	*
2000	Misty Sunset	*
3200	Solid Gold	*

CABLE		
001P	Silver	*
002P	Gold	*

PLASTIC CANVAS THREAD GUIDE

Thread Size	7 Count Canvas	10 Count Canvas	14 Count Canvas
Fine (#8) Braid			Full cross
Tapestry (#12) Braid			Full cross
Medium (#16) Braid		Half cross continental (double strand)	Half cross continental
Heavy (#32) Braid		Half cross continental	
⅛" Ribbon	Full cross	Half cross continental	
1⁄16" Ribbon	Full cross	Full cross	Half cross continental

GLOSSARY

ASSISI WORK
A technique where the background is stitched and the subject motifs are left unworked but frequently outlined, causing them to appear as voids on the embroidery. Outlining with metallic threads creates a unique definition and distinction to Assisi patterns.

AWL
A pointed instrument for piercing and enlarging small holes to enable easy thread passage.

BENT WEAVER'S NEEDLE
A laying tool which is a 9–10cm (3½–4in) tapestry needle with a bent tip. The bent tip allows the stitcher to separate and lay threads without having the fingers or hand touch the fabric (ground).

BLACKWORK
A classic embroidery style used to imitate lace. It dates back to the fourteenth century and became very fashionable in the court of Henry VIII of England during the sixteenth century. The use of metallic threads in blackwork today has become increasingly important because it offers the stitcher many more opportunities to vary the density and tone of the patterns while still creating the delicacy noted in fine lace.

BODKIN
A flat, smooth and narrow 9–10cm (3½–4in) plastic or metal laying tool.

COUCHING
A method of attaching threads to the surface of embroidery (see page 37).

DIMENSION
Any measurable extent, as length, width, depth, etc. scope or importance; the nature and relationship of the parts to the whole entering into some physical quantity; dimensional – having dimensions.

DEPTH
The distance from the top downward; intensity, such as in colours, silence and emotion; creation of a third dimension in appearance.

FILLET
In picture framing a fillet is a small moulding inside the edge of a frame. The same effect may be achieved by using different metallic threads and trims that serve as the fillet between the embroidery and the edge of the frame.

GROUND
The fabric or canvas on which an embroidery is stitched.

LAYING TOOL
A tool, the proper use of which assists the stitcher in keeping multiple strands of thread parallel and smooth during the stitching process. Properly laid threads reflect the maximum amount of light and provide a uniform appearance to the embroidery. Laying tools include a large tapestry or rug needle, bodkin, trolley needle, teko-bari and bent weaver's needle. See teko-bari below.

LUMINOUS
Giving off light; shining bright; filled with light.

OVERSTITCHING
This is stitching a different thread on top of a stitch already in place.

PLUNGING
The process of sinking and securing the beginning and ends of surface threads to the back of the embroidery (see page 37).

TEKO-BARI
This is a Japanese laying tool properly called a stroking needle. It is a 10cm (4in) stiletto-shaped metal tool with an extra fine point to separate threads, particularly suited for laying filament silk.

TEXTURE

The characteristic, visual and tactile quality of the surface of a work of art resulting from the way in which the materials are used. A rough or grainy surface, smooth or patterned.

TROLLEY NEEDLE

A large tapestry needle attached to a finger guard for convenience. The trolley needle is placed on a finger of the non-dominant hand for easy use. (You **must** remember that you have the trolley needle on before raising your hand to your face.)

TWIST

The direction of two or more strands of threads winding together.

WASTE KNOT

A method of starting off thread, with two main types – an in-line waste knot and an away waste knot (see page 31).

WHIPSTITCHING

A method of joining or finishing, where stitches are sewn or passed over fabric edges.

BIBLIOGRAPHY

AMBUTER, Carolyn, Carolyn Ambuter's Even More Complete Book of Needlepoint (Harper & Row, New York 1987)

BISHOP, Emie, Embellishments No.96. Cross 'n Patch (Millville, Utah 1994)

BURNHAM, Sophy, A Book of Angels (Ballantine Books, New York 1990)

CAMPBELL-HARDING, Valerie, LEMON, Jane and PYMAN, Kit, Goldwork (Search Press Limited, UK 1995)

DEAN, Beryl, Ecclesiastical Embroidery (Batsford, London 1958)

DRYSDALE, Rosemary, The Art of Blackwork Embroidery (Charles Scribner's Sons, New York 1975)

GAWAIN, Shakti, Creative Visualization (Bantam Books, New York 1982)

HANDELL, Albert and TRAINOR HANDELL, Leslie, Intuitive Light (Watson-Guptill Publications, New York 1995)

KREINIK, Metallic Ribbon Embroidery (Little Rock, AR: Leisure Arts Leaflet No.2893, 1996)

KREINIK, Andrew, 'Kreinik: 25th Anniversary' (in New Stitches Faversham, Kent, England 1997)

KREINIK, Jacqueline Friedman, 'The Magic of Metallic and Metal Threads' (in Just Cross Stitch, Peoria, Illinois: Symbols of Excellence Publishers, PJS Publications, September/October 1995)

KREINIK, Jerry and KREINIK, Jacqueline, 'Black Magic Butterfly' (in The Cross Stitcher, Clapper Communications Inc., October 1996)

LEMON, Jane, Metal Thread Embroidery (Batsford, London 1987)

PASCOE, Margaret, Blackwork Embroidery (P.T. Batsford Ltd., London 1986)

PIZZUTO J. J., Fabric Science (6th Edition, Edited by Arthur Price and Allen C. Cohen. Fairchild Publications, New York 1994)

PYMAN, Kit, Gold and Silver Embroidery (Search Press, UK 1987)

ROGERS, Sandy, Silk and Metal Threads on Canvas (Expanded Edition. Ohio: The Yarn Cellar Publishing Company 1995)

SWIFT, Gay, The Batsford Encyclopaedia of Embroidery Techniques (B.T. Batsford Ltd., London 1984)

TORTORA, Phillis G., Understanding Textiles (3rd Edition MacMillan Publishing Company, New York 1987)

WARK, Edna, Metal Thread Embroidery (Kangaroo Press, London 1958)

WILD, John Peter, Textiles in Archaeology (Shire Publications, Ltd., UK 1988)

ZIMMERMAN, Jane, 'What are Metal Threads?' (in NeedlePointers Vol.26, No. 4, July 1998)

ZIMMERMAN, Jane. The Canvas Work Encyclopaedia (Richmond, CA: self-published, 1989)

SUPPLIERS

US SUPPLIERS

Anchor Threads from
Coats & Clark
P.O. Box 12229
Greenville, SC 29612-0229
Tel: (800) 648-1479
www.coatsandclark.com
*For threads and a wide
range of needlework
supplies*

Caron International Yarns
US contact: Ed Hamrick
Caron P.O. Box 222
Washington, NC 27889
Tel: 800 868 9190
Fax: 252 975 7309
www.hamrick@caron.com
For threads

Charles Crafts, Inc.
P.O. Box 1049
Laurinburg, NC 28353
Consumer Line
Tel: 1-800-277-0980
www.charlescraft.com
*For fabric, threads and a
wide range of needle-
work supplies and the
acrylic mug used in
Fantasy Cove (E-Z Stitch
#VC-2010-6755)*

Darice
21160 Drake Road
Strongsville, Ohio 44136
Tel: 1-440-238-9150
Fax: 1-440-238-8320
www.Darice.com
For plastic canvas

DMC Corporation
10 Port Kearny
South Kearny, NJ 07032
Tel: 1-973-589-0606
Fax: 1-973-589-8931
www.DMC-USA.com
*For fabrics, threads and a
wide range of needle-
work supplies*

**Kreinik Manufacturing Co.,
Inc.**
3106 Timanus Lane,
Suite 101
Baltimore, Maryland 21244
Consumer Line
Tel: 1-800-537-2166
Tel: 1-410-281-0040
Fax: 1-410-281-0987
www.Kreinik.com
*For metallic and silk
threads*

Lee's Needlearts, Inc.
5630 East Route 38
Pennsauken, NJ 08109
Tel: 1-609-665-8323
Fax: 1-609-665-3812
*For a wide range of
needlework supplies*

Sudberry House
12 Colton Road
P.O. Box 895
Old Lyme, CT 06371
www.sudberry.com
*For the box used in
Dragonfly Illusion
(Sudberry box #991782
medium oak with white-
wash finish)*

Zweigart Fabrics
From Joan Toggit, Ltd.
2 Riverview Drive
Somerset, NJ 08873-1139
Tel: 1-732-271-1949
Fax: 1-732-271-0758
www.Zweigart.com
For embroidery fabrics

UK SUPPLIERS

Coats Craft UK
P.O. Box 22
The Lingfield Estate
McMullen Road,
Darlington, County
Durham DL1 1YQ
Tel: 01325 365457
Fax: 01325 394200
*For a wide range of
needlework supplies (and
mugs for stitching, e.g. as
in Fantasy Cove)*

Darice plastic canvas
available from:
Hobby Craft
Tel: 0800 0272387
www.hobbycraft.com

DMC Creative World
Pullman Road, Wigston
Leicestershire LE18 2DY
Tel: 0116 281 1040
Fax: 0116 281 3592
*For fabrics, threads and a
wide range of needle-
work supplies*

Framecraft Miniatures Ltd
372–376 Summer Lane
Hockley, Birmingham B19
3QA
Tel: 0121 212 0551
Fax: 0121 212 0552
*For a wide range of
needlework supplies –
fabric, threads, Mill Hill
beads*

Hantex Ltd
Unit 8–9, Lodge Farm
Units
Wolverton Road,
Castelthorpe
Buckinghamshire MK19
7ES
Tel: 01908 511428
*For Mill Hill beads and
other needlework
embellishments*

ACKNOWLEDGEMENTS

This book was not accomplished in isolation. Many talented individuals contributed to the effort and acknowledgements go to a very diverse and gifted group.

I would like to thank all the designers who created inspiring designs that captured the essence of using our premium speciality threads. It is through designs that we learn how to stitch and appreciate the unique properties of threads. These threads, manufactured by Kreinik in West Virginia, undergo close scrutiny by Douglas Kreinik and Gladys Lemley so that all threads are consistent in quality and meet the rigorous high standards established by Kreinik Manufacturing Co., Inc.

Gratitude goes to Dena Lenham of Kreinik. Her background in embroidery coupled with her precise skills in English and journalism helped keep the book grammatically correct and the words flowing smoothly.

A generous thank you goes to Linda Burkett, an avid needlewoman who strives for excellence with each stitch in every design. Her feedback kept all focused on explaining the necessary basic techniques that form the foundation for learning all the valuable hints for using these threads.

To Linda Clements who earned my deep appreciation as an objective and valued editor: her understanding of our mission and enthusiasm for this project was immediate and gratifying.

Special acknowledgement and deep gratitude go to Ann Caswell, design co-ordinator and teacher. Ann's outstanding abilities as a teacher, needlewoman and communicator helped co-ordinate the many aspects of the book. Ann's love for needlework and her passionate desire to create 'teachable moments' resulted in a clear and concise format that will enable the reader to learn. Thank you, Ann.

Ann wishes to thank Beth Robertson for her assistance. Beth's help with some of the graphics and her scans of line drawings were invaluable in meeting the deadlines. Ann also wishes to thank her husband, Kaz, for his help and advice and for his seemingly unlimited patience throughout the process.

And of course, special acknowledgements go to my husband and partner, Andrew. He read every word carefully and offered constructive criticism to clarify the book and benefit the reader. I also want to thank my ten-year-old son, Zachary. He understood my need for quiet, uninterrupted work time at home and he offered his smiling face as encouragement.

Lastly, I want to thank Estelle and Jerry Kreinik, co-founders of Kreinik Manufacturing Co., Inc. and innovative leaders in the field of embroidery. Their contribution to needlework made this publication necessary and valuable.

FINISHERS

Acknowledgements go to the following people for their skilled work in finishing and making up the projects.

'Friendship Angel' – Bette Tippett, Traveling Threads, San Jose, California.

'Poppies, Snails and Peacocks' Tails' – Marcia Brown, The Binding Stitch, Dennis, Massachusetts.

'Sleeping Mermaid and Rainbow Fishes' – Marcia Brown, The Binding Stitch, Dennis, Massachusetts.

'Classic Golden Balantine' – Inge Ruiseco Sterling, Virginia.

'Regency Stocking' – Eleanor Podl, Saskatchewan, Canada.

INDEX

Illustrations *italic*   Stitch diagrams/charts **bold**